GW00786313

Institute of Management Consultants & Advisers

Directory 2007

INSTITUTE OF MANAGEMENT CONSULTANTS & ADVISERS
One Spencer Dock, North Wall Quay, Dublin 1, Ireland

© 2007 Institute of Management Consultants & Advisers

A catalogue record of this book is
available from the British Library.

ISBN 978-0-9556959-02

All rights reserved.
No part of this publication may be reproduced or transmitted in
any form or by any means, including photocopying and
recording, without written permission of the publisher.
Such written permission must also be obtained before any part of
this publication is stored in a retrieval system of any nature.
Requests for permission should be directed to
Institute of Management Consultants & Advisers
One Spencer Dock, North Wall Quay, Dublin 1, Ireland.

Prepared by IMCA Editorial Panel:
Ken Germaine, Krishna De, Colm Ó Maolmhuire, Brian O'Kane.
Designed & typeset by Oak Tree Press.

Printed in Ireland by Colour Books Limited.

CONTENTS

Introduction

The IMCA is a new Institute, formed by the merger of the IMCI and the Irish branch of the IBA. Since its formation in 2006, the Institute has developed a large membership base within the three main constituencies of the profession, namely: the members of medium to large consultancy firms, members from smaller consultancy firms and members who work in public sector and third sector organisations.

The strategic vision of the IMCA is to become the primary representative body for the management consultancy and business advice profession in the Republic of Ireland. We are implementing a strategic plan to achieve this.

The management consulting and advisory profession plays a vital part in the development of our country, to enable it to compete where it matters. This purpose of this new Directory to provide a valuable reference source of information for clients, potential clients, members and prospective members.

Should readers require any further information, I would be delighted if you would contact me or any of the officers of the IMCA.

Best wishes
David W Duffy
President IMCA

Institute of Management Consultants & Advisers

IMCA came into being on 1 March 2006, following a merger of the memberships of the Institute of Management Consultants in Ireland (IMCI) and the Republic of Ireland Branch of the Institute of Business Advisers (IBA).

IMCI was incorporated in 1980 and operated as a regional branch of the UK Institute until 1994. On 1 January 1995, it became an autonomous Institute for the profession in Ireland.

The IBA was set up in Ireland in 1998 to service the needs of the Business Advisory Community, public and private. The IBA operated as a Regional branch of the IBA and cooperated closely with the branch in Northern Ireland.

The principal objective of IMCA is the advancement of the professions of management consultancy and business advice, through the establishment and maintenance of the highest standards of performance and conduct by its members, and by the promotion of the knowledge and skills required for that purpose. Membership is open to individual management consultants and business advisers and embraces consultants and advisers working with major international practices, specialist sole practitioners and those operating in State agencies.

Membership

There are five grades of membership within IMCA – Associate Member, Member, Fellow, Student and Retired. The entry requirements for each of these are set out below.

To become an **Associate Member**, you must:

- Hold a degree or equivalent professional qualification (other than in exceptional cases).
- Be engaged full-time in management consultancy or business advisory services.

To become a **Member**, you must:

- Have three years' full-time experience as Management Consultant or Business Adviser, **or**
- Have three years' experience in a practice with IMCA-recognised training arrangements.
- Hold a degree or equivalent professional qualification as issued by recognised institute, or experience in lieu.
- Be engaged full-time in management consultancy or business advisory services.

Qualifying Members may also apply to become a Certified Management Consultant (see below).

To become a **Fellow**, you must have been a Member for five years; it is not possible to join IMCA direct as a Fellow.

IMCA recognises a grade of **Student Member** from the MBS in Management Consultancy awarded by the Michael Smurfit Business School, and may recognise other courses as also being appropriate from time to time. Applications for Student Membership must be countersigned by the Administrator of the post-graduate programme.

Retired members are former members who wish to maintain that links with the Institute.

Practices

Accredited Consulting Practices are larger management consultancy practices, whose training and other arrangements for the development of consultants working for their firms have been approved by IMCA. These practices are managed by Members and undertake to adhere to IMCA's Code of Professional Conduct.

Registered Consulting Practices are consultancy organisations that are managed by Members or Fellows of the Institute who are Certified Management Consultants (CMC), and which undertake to adhere to IMCA's Code of Professional Conduct.

Independent Consultants & Advisers

Independent Consultants and Advisers are individual management consultants and business advisers, who have amassed substantial experience and specialist expertise. Within his/her field of work and expertise, a Member can offer many benefits to clients.

Certified Management Consultants

IMCA is authorised to award the Certified Management Consultant (CMC) designation in Ireland. CMC is an internationally-recognised management consultancy qualification based on strict certification requirements relating to competence, ethics and independence. Only members of the International Council of Management Consulting Institutes (ICMCI) can award the CMC qualification.

Individuals can apply directly to IMCA to become an Associate as the precursor to securing CMC, or they can work towards CMC as a consequence of being employed within an Accredited Practice.

IMCA Officers & Council 2007

President	**David Duffy** Prospectus Management Consultants
Vice-President	**Willie Maxwell** InterTradeIreland / Acumen
Joint Treasurers	**Rex Coghlan** Visible Business Advice
	Tom Hynes Deloitte
Company Secretary	**Brian Flanagan** Invest-Tech
Directors	**Miriam Ahern** Align Management Solutions
	Laura Curtin Observer for Southern Region
	Assunta Delany FÁS
	Jim Fitzsimons Riverwest Management
	Ken Germaine Independent Consultants & Advisers Group
	Paraic Hegarty Chaos Management

Michael Lenahan
ESCA

Mary McEntee
Zilcom Systems

Breda McNally
Training & Evaluation Services

Tom Moriarty
MDR Consulting

Tom Murray
FGS

Pat Nolan
Facit Consulting

Gerry O'Carroll
Watson Wyatt

Bernard O'Rourke
PERFORM Management Consultants

Padraig Warren
Padraig Warren & Associates

Using & Choosing Management Consultants

Why Use Consultants?

In today's intensely competitive international trading environment, the number of factors with which management must deal has increased dramatically and the speed of change is accelerating all the time. Changes in the domestic economy, the economies and politics of other countries, social legislation and the impact of new technology all bring with them challenges and opportunities calling for knowledge and expertise, not always readily available within an organisation. To meet these challenges and to grasp the opportunities, organisations call in management consultants from time to time for specific assignments as part of normal management practice, in just the same way as architects, designers and always have always been engaged when the need arises.

In whatever assignment involved, the management consultant brings four resources that cannot be combined in any other manner:

- **Objectivity:** There is no real alternative to the independent, impartial, fresh viewpoint, free of personal interest, pre-conceptions or existing traditions or loyalties.

- **Broad experience:** Management consultants working with a wide variety of clients frequently tackle problems that confront any individual client only once in a decade or more.

- **Analytical skill:** Management consultants are trained in a range of analytical skills and know how to concentrate on the main problem areas and define the requirements for solution and benefits to be gained.

- **Full-time attention:** Consultants can devote full-time attention to the assignment, free of the executive responsibilities of client managers.

When to Use a Management Consultant

The need to engage a management consultant may arise when:

- A problem is known to exist, but the organisation does not have the time, the particular experience or the staff to tackle it.

- A problem is known to exist, but neither the symptoms nor the underlying cause can be determined by anyone in the organisation in a completely unbiased way.

- The organisation has tackled the problem itself already, but has not resolved it.

- Expertise is needed to introduce new technology, new techniques and / or fundamental change in the organisation's structure, nature or direction.

- A conflict of views on future policy exists within the organisation and an independent and skilled assessment is needed.

- A specialist sort of experience or expertise is required, which does not exist within the organisation, and secondment of a management consultant for a period can help to determine the type of permanent staff to be required.

- An appraisal of proposed changes is needed to confirm and / or amend the organisation's plans and help implement them.

- In the smaller organisation, there is a need to import a particular type of knowledge or expertise for a period to deal with such matters as market research, product development or diversification, industrial design or engineering, etc.

Selecting a Management Consultant

So how does an organisation choose a management consultant – especially when doing so for the first time – so as to ensure that the selection produces a properly qualified, sound professional? There are number of steps to consider.

Defining the problem

- Describe the job you want done and specify the things you want from the assignment.
- Understand precisely how you expect your business will benefit from the work.
- Decide on the timescale, scope and any constraints on the assignment.
- Clarify which key staff (including yourself) will be involved, and how their time will be made available.
- Consult any fellow directors / key managers on the nature of the problem (where appropriate).
- Define the expertise you want – is it a systems or human problem, as you perceive it?

Choosing the consultant

- Properly brief the consultants asked to quote – give them all background to your definition of the problem. Otherwise, you will get proposals that don't meet your requirements.
- Make sure you only ask consultants to quote for the work who are qualified to carry it out. The Institute of Management Consultants & Advisers has a Code of Conduct that requires members not to take on assignments for which they are not qualified.
- If you do not know a suitable consultant, ask the Institute of Management Consultants & Advisers. It has a free enquiry service that can put you in contact with a number of qualified consultants or consultancy practices.

- Ask possible consultants to send you their CVs or to come to talk to you about the task – they should do this free of charge.
- Consultancy is a people-driven service – make sure that the "chemistry" between you and the consultant is right and that you meet the person who is going to do the work.
- Ask short-listed consultants (two or three maximum) to provide you with a detailed written proposal covering:
    o   Their understanding of the problem.
    o   Terms of reference.
    o   The names and CVs of the consultants who will do the work.
    o   Other support provided by the firm.
    o   The workplan and timescale.
    o   The reports and / or systems that will be delivered to you.
    o   Fees and expenses and schedule of payment.
    o   The inputs required from you.
- If you are not happy with any of the proposals, do not feel pressured into accepting one – go back to the starting point or discuss with the consultants.
- Remember the cheapest will not necessarily give the best value for money.
- Talk through your chosen proposals with the consultant before making a final decision, to ensure that you have any concerns answered and obtain references.

Ten Golden Rules

- Describe the job you want done and the things you **expect** from the assignment, as well as the expertise you require.
- **Consult** with others in your organisation.
- **Brief** the consultants properly – with all pertinent facts.
- Meet the **individual** consultant who will do the job and make sure the "chemistry" between you is right.
- Ask no more than **three** short-listed consultants to provide detailed written proposals.
- Ask for **references** and follow them up.
- Keep **in touch** with the progress of the assignment.
- The final report should contain **no surprises**.
- Aim to get your own staff to "buy in" or "**own**" the recommendations – involve them as early as possible.
- Be prepared to **implement** the recommendations – and involve your management, as well as the consultant.

IMCA Code of Conduct

IMCA's Code of Professional Conduct is structured on three basic principles, dealing with:

- Meeting the client's requirements
- Integrity, independence, objectivity.
- Responsibility to the profession and the Institute.

Confidentiality

A member will treat client information as confidential and will neither take personal advantage of privileged information gathered during an assignment, nor enable others to do so.

Unrealistic Expectations

A member will refrain from encouraging unrealistic expectations or promising clients that benefits are certain from specific management consulting and advisory services. A member will ensure that before accepting any engagement, a mutual understanding of the objectives, scope, workplan, and fee arrangements has been established with the client. A member will advise the client of any significant reservations the member may have about the client's expectation of benefits from an engagement.

Commissions / Financial Interests

A member will neither accept commissions, remuneration nor other benefits from a third party in connection with recommendations to a client without the client's knowledge and consent nor fail to disclose any financial interest in goods or services which form part of such recommendations.

Assignments

A member will only accept work that the member is qualified to perform and in which the client can be served effectively; a member will not make any misleading claims and will provide references from other clients, if requested.

Disclosure & Conflicts of Interest

A member will disclose at the earliest opportunity any special relationships, circumstances or business interests which might influence or impair, or could be seen by the client or others to influence or impair, the member's judgement or objectivity on a particular assignment. This requires the prior disclosure of all relevant personal, financial or other business interests that could not be inferred from the description of the services offered. In particular, this relates to:

- Any directorship or controlling interest in any business in competition with the client.
- Any financial interest in goods or services recommended or supplied to the client.
- Any personal relationship with any individual in the client's employ.
- Any personal investment in the client organisation or in its parent or any subsidiary companies.
- Any recent or current engagements in sensitive areas of work with directly competitive clients.
- Any work for a third party on the opposite side of a transaction – for example, bid defence, acquisitions, work for the regulator and the regulated, assessing the products of an existing client.

A member will not serve a client under circumstances that are inconsistent with the member's professional obligations or that in any way might be seen to impair the member's integrity; wherever a conflict or potential conflict of interest arises, the member will, as the circumstances require, either withdraw from the assignment, remove the source of conflict or disclose and obtain the agreement of the parties concerned to the performance or continuance of the engagement.

Recruiting

A member will not make offers of employment to or engage any member of the client's staff nor use the services of any such person either independently or via a third party unless they have first obtained the client's written consent.

Standards of Service

A member will carry out the duties, which he or she has undertaken for his/her client diligently, conscientiously and with due regard to his/her client's interest. A member will maintain a fully professional approach in all dealings with clients, the general public and fellow members.

Personal Conduct

A member shall be a fit and proper person to carry on the profession of management consultancy and advisory services and shall at all times be of good reputation and character.

Particular matters for concern might include:

- Conviction of a criminal offence or committal under bankruptcy proceedings.
- Censure or disciplining by a court or regulatory authority.
- Unethical or improper behaviour towards employees or the general public

A member shall not wilfully give IMCA false, inaccurate, misleading or incomplete information.

Other Management Consultants

A member will ensure that other management consultants and advisers carrying out work on behalf of the member are conversant with, and abide by, this Code of Professional Conduct. A member will sub-contract work only with the prior agreement of the client and, except where otherwise agreed, will remain responsible for the performance of the work.

Issue No. 4, 16 August 2006.

IMCA ETHICAL GUIDELINES

In recent years, the perceived lack of individual ethical behaviour in business has received increasing publicity and scrutiny in the media. The public response has been an increased level of expectations of higher standards from public servants, elected representatives and professional advisors.

IMCA has published these guidelines to assist members and to provide some tests that can be used to gauge the extent, or otherwise, of members' ethical behaviour.

IMCA's Code of Conduct is founded on three basic principles, namely:

- Meeting the client's requirements.
- Integrity, independence, objectivity.
- Responsibility to the profession and the Institute.

This guidance describes two additional principles that should attach to an ethical decision, and sets out a number of questions designed to assist individual members to gain an objective insight to their quandary. Having considered these questions, a member may feel the need to discuss the problem with someone else, and IMCA will provide access to such support.

This service, which is free and without commitment, and which is aimed at assisting the member to develop their own resolution, is described at the conclusion of these guidelines.

Basic Guidelines

A member should consider, with these guidelines, the interests of a wider number and range of 'stakeholders'. 'Stakeholders' has become common usage in ethical circles to refer to those individuals or organisations that have an interest or stake in the situation. Stakeholders may include the general public and the national interest.

Two basic touchstones or tests to use are transparency and vulnerability. Transparency means the degree to which there is openness in the situation, that is, how much knowledge or information has been made available to the stakeholders. If there is not full and complete openness, the reason for such lack of transparency should be carefully examined by the member. Vulnerability refers to the extent to which each of the stakeholders' interests are at risk as a result of the proposed action (or inaction). It may be that a client or a third party is vulnerable because of ignorance, incompetence or financial weakness. A member must give due weight to stakeholders' interests before acting. However, the client comes first, and a member's ethical concerns and any resulting actions must be explained to the client.

Below are some questions designed to assist individual members to consider how to deal with an ethical problem. They are not equally applicable to every situation and discretion should be exercised in selecting those that are relevant.

Background

It is important to try to place dilemmas in context, and the initial questions are designed to obtain facts about the situation.

1.   *Have you defined the circumstances accurately?* Have you examined other issues which may be less tangible and less easy to evaluate, such as the motives or aims of stakeholders, which may have a bearing on the influences involved.

2.   *How did this situation occur?* Again, the circumstances surrounding the events leading up to the present

situation need to be considered carefully. This can be helpful in determining the motives of those involved.

3.   *What is your role in this situation?* Have you contributed to the circumstances wittingly or unwittingly? What have you to gain/lose? What do others in the situation think is your role? Note that if you have a stake in the situation, you are probably breaking the Code of Conduct.

4.   *How does your intention compare with the probable results?* The answer to this question may lay bare the real core of the dilemma – how will you appear to your peers, the public, and the other stakeholders? Should you be influenced by such a consideration? Perhaps, by the very act of your decision becoming public, the nature of the dilemma changes, and this leads to another question:

5.   *Are you confident that your position is as valid over a long period of time, as it seems now?* With the passage of time, the dilemma may disappear, or it may be exacerbated. Perhaps the potential action (or inaction) will add to the complexity or introduce new factors. Will the solution still seem relevant?

6.   *Under what conditions would you allow exceptions to your stand?* If you can arrive at an acceptable solution (in your judgement), it may be that there can, and should, be exceptions. You must be careful about such a conclusion, since it is then a very short step to justifying a self-serving decision, on the basis that you are the exception.

Up to this point, you will be acting not unlike the way a professional management consultant should. Namely, independently and objectively establishing the facts of the situation and bringing to bear an informed and experienced judgement. This process itself may bring a different perspective to the matter, which may result in the potential dilemma dissolving without further action. The very act of seeking objective facts may expose the core of the problem and thus its potential resolution.

Some consultants may find that progressing each of these questions with a trusted colleague or associate may help to clarify the answers and make the action to be taken easier to identify.

However, the clearer understanding obtained as a result of your self-questioning may serve to heighten the dilemma and expose a difficult challenge. The following questions are suggested to help you formulate a solution.

Vulnerabilities

1. *What options do you have? As an advisor?* It is important to attempt to see the situation as objectively as possible. Yet, this may be difficult since ethical dilemmas, by their nature, are not normally publicised, and it is not normally practical to talk the issue over with a third party. Because you are probably the only one in the possession of all the facts and who understands that a dilemma exists, you are almost certainly the only one who can understand what options there are.

2. *What opportunities do you have to discuss the issue with a colleague or third party?* If you are a sole practitioner or part of a small firm, you can be more vulnerable than if you work in a larger firm. If you have such opportunities, you can test your opinion against a knowledgeable trusted colleague.

3. *What are the consequences for each stakeholder of your action – or equally important – inaction?* The consequences may be apparent but sometimes they are not easy to design. There may be damaging consequences, no matter what course of action is taken, and the dilemma rests in making a decision that results in the least damage (at least, in your judgement).

4. *To whom and what do you give your loyalty as a person and as a member of the organisation?* Often the dilemma is coloured, or at least tinged, with personal and / or poor 'client' relationship. In business, one must make

decisions, which can affect careers and which can be seen to be disloyal or even hostile to a particular superior. This may result in an uncomfortable working environment, and could contribute to the nature of one's decision.

5.   *Could your actions withstand cross-examination in court by an eminent barrister?* This question is proposed as the strictest of all public credibility tests.

This second group of questions is aimed at helping individual members to formulate an objective understanding of their quandary and to understand where the vulnerabilities lie.

The next few questions are focussed differently and are concerned with transparency. If you feel uncomfortable about any of the answers, you should probe more deeply into the reason(s) for this.

Transparency

1.   *Can you discuss the problem with the client before you make the decision?* The answer to this question indicates to what extent the principles of transparency are present. If there are any circumstances existing that make such a discussion unlikely, you need to consider why this is so. Is it possible that such a discussion perhaps could expose something with which you are uncomfortable or even weaken your legal position?

2.   *Would you feel comfortable explaining your behaviour to your family? Your friends? Your fellow workers?* The purpose of this question is to explore the degree of comfort you have with your behaviour. If you feel uncomfortable with the answer, you must seriously question your behaviour.

3.   *Would you feel comfortable if your actions were announced on television or printed in a newspaper?* Although you may feel comfortable with handling your family and friends, you may still be uncomfortable when faced with the

possibility of having to explain your actions in the media. Does this have a bearing on your behaviour?

4.   *Would you feel confident that the action you propose to take (or not to take) would be viewed as proper by your peers?* While you may be confident that you can rationalise and explain your actions to your family, your friends, the stakeholders and to the media, what about your professional peers? They are more likely to understand the issues involved and to be able to form an informed point of view.

Conclusion

Members are responsible for their own actions, and these testing questions are offered as guidance for members to help in forming their own opinion. The questions are not exhaustive or exclusive, and other questions may suggest themselves during the course of working through the process.

For further confidential advice, contact the President of IMCA, who may refer you to a confidential contact. If you decide to do so, you will be asked for the following information on a confidential basis:

- The names of the parties involved (to ensure that conflicts of interest are excluded).
- The nature of the work involved and your role in that work.
- An outline of the issue.
- The time-scale involved (is it urgent?).
- What sort of guidance you are seeking.
- Confirmation that you wish the President to approach the confidential contact.

An independent panel member will be selected, who will contact the member to define the problem and offer assistance – usually by phone. Other panel members will be involved, if required, and subject to the member's agreement.

The panel will aim to help the member come to his/her own resolution of the matter, and under no circumstances can the Institute or panel member accept responsibility for the consequence of members' actions.

Issue No. 2, 1 May 2006.

CMC COMPETENCY FRAMEWORK

A Certified Management Consultant (CMC) is a management consultant who meets these 'core competences', as explained overleaf:

- Values and behavioural skills.
- Technical, consultancy and specialisation skills.
- Business insight.

Members who are Certified Management Consultants are identified in the Directory sections by the CMC designation.

CMC Competency Framework

Major	Sub-set	Components	Definition
VALUES & BEHAVIOURS	Ethics & Professionalism	Values, ethics & professionalism	Adheres to code of conduct and ethical guidelines. Demonstrates professional integrity, consistency, transparency, accountability, responsibility and reliability.
	Analytical skills	Observations & analysis	Recommendations are supported by objective facts and research.
		Conceptualisation & problem solving	Employs structured approaches to generate ideas, evaluate and select options.
		Complexity, change & diversity	Understands complexity of operating environment and impact of selected course of actions on others.
	Personal Interaction	Communication & presentation	Uses a range of techniques and approaches to convey thoughts and ideas in a range of situations
		Responsibility & accountability	Responsible for own actions, demonstrating resilience, drive and commitment to results.
		Influencing	Presents ideas convincingly to produce specific outcomes.
	Personal development	Focus and time management	Delivers timely solutions, balancing priorities and managing time effectively.
		Self development	Proven track record of self development and personal growth. Proven ability to learn from past assignments and apply knowledge.

Major	Sub-set	Components	Definition
TECHNICAL COMPETENCE	**Functional specialisation**	Knowledge and skill	Recognised as an expert in own discipline, applying expertise in one or more industry sectors
		Client focus	Scopes client requirements, presenting clear comprehensive proposals. Identifies and articulates project drivers, strategic fit and commercial benefits with client in respect of one or more individual projects. Understand client cultures, addresses client satisfaction; understand client motivation impacts
	Consulting skills	Project management	Manages client projects effectively- setting objectives, deadlines and budgets, using appropriate project management tools and methodologies and ensuring seamless withdrawal process.
		Consultative process	Uses a range of techniques, including facilitation, to deliver solutions of mutual benefit.
		Knowledge	Captures, shares and applies knowledge in a structured way, relevant to the engagement needs
		Partnering and networking	Leverages network effectively to engage expertise of others, developing others as appropriate
		Tools and methodologies	Selects and uses an appropriate range of tools and methodologies

Major	Sub-set	Components	Definition
		Risk and quality management	Defines quality standards, ensuring quality of delivery and client satisfaction. Defines risk criteria, identifying, mitigating and managing risks and outcomes.
	Consulting business knowledge	Consultancy business knowledge	Understands the nature of the management consultancy market, competitors and capabilities.
		Commercial aspects of assignments	Demonstrates understanding of commercial aspects of project including scope, risk, terms and conditions and pricing.
BUSINESS INSIGHT	Breadth of knowledge	External awareness	Demonstrates understanding of political, economic, social, technological, legal and environmental factors (PESTLE) impacting on area of work.
		Business knowledge	Understands business structures. processes, management and disciplines and impact on own area of work.
		Understanding the client	Has researched and understood client business operations and agenda.

Based on ICMCI Professional standards – Part 2: Competencies & Definitions, updated 20 January 2005.
Issue No. 2, 1 May 2006.

IMCA SERVICES TO MEMBERS

IMCA offers a range of services and special offers to members, full details of which are available on the Institute's website, including:

- **Towergate Professional Risks:** IMCA has negotiated a very attractive deal on **professional indemnity insurance**. Towergate Professional Risks, based in Leeds, are the broker managing the scheme and Royal Sun Alliance are the insurers. The scheme offers a simple application process with immediate cover and very competitive rates.

- **Bank of Ireland:** Bank of Ireland is pleased to provide IMCA members with a range of **financial offers**, including a free personal financial review, free banking for current account holders and a range of savings options. It is not necessary to be an Account Holder with Bank of Ireland to avail of these preferential offers.

- **First Active:** IMCA, in conjunction with Friends First Finance Ltd., has put together a **finance plan** for members who wish to fund the cost of professional indemnity insurance, preliminary tax, pension contributions or other personal or business-related expenditure. As an IMCA member, you may qualify for an unsecured personal loan, up to €20,000, through Friends First Finance Direct, at the following preferential terms: low APR of 8.5% fixed, no early settlement penalties, no set-up/administration fees, and same day processing and funds advance.

- **Glennon Insurance Brokers & Consultants:** IMCA has negotiated **Drivesure and Homesure,** two new insurance schemes for insuring the cars and homes of members and their spouses or partners, offering competitive rates, broad cover, premium payment by installment, and ease and simplicity in arranging the policies. The schemes are insured with Allianz Corporate Ireland Plc.

- **PlanWare:** PlanWare offers a 20% discount to IMCA members on its Exl-Plan and Cashflow Plan **business-related financial and cashflow planners**. These Excel-based programmes are available in a range of versions to suit most types of new and established businesses. They are widely used by consultants and advisers to generate fully-integrated, comprehensive financial projections for clients for business planning, strategy development and raising finance. PlanWare also offers a 10% discount on the Plan Write and Insight ranges of business, marketing and strategic planning software.

- **VIVAS Health Group Scheme:** IMCA has a group scheme with **VIVAS Health** and, as an IMCA member, you qualify for a 10% group discount.

- *Business & Finance* **magazine:** *Business & Finance* has agreed to provide a €90 reduction on the **annual subscription** price to IMCA members, reducing it to €69.69. Your subscription to *Business & Finance* will be delivered by post direct to you every fortnight, prior to its availability on the News stands.

- **Oak Tree Press:** Oak Tree Press are Ireland's leading **business book** publisher, with a wide range of titles on human resources, starting and growing a business, accounting and finance, sales, marketing and law. Oak Tree is offering a 20% reduction to IMCA members on all titles.

- **Bar Council Direct Professional Access:** The Bar Council of Ireland has authorised IMCA as an Approved Organisation under the Direct Professional Access Scheme, which allows IMCA members direct access to members of the services of barristers in non-contentious matters (situations that do not involve a court visit). IMCA members can now instruct barristers directly without the requirement first to consult a solicitor, in non-contentious situations. This can be very useful where a member requires a legal opinion on a business matter concerning the interpretation of the law, contracts or agreements. Fees payable to barristers are a matter for negotiation between the member and the barrister.

Please note that the products and services listed above are provided for the convenience of members and does not imply any endorsement of the products and services by IMCA.

ACCREDITED CONSULTING PRACTICES

Accredited Consulting Practices are larger management consultancy practices, whose training and other arrangements for the development of consultants working for their firms have been approved by IMCA. They are managed by IMCA Members and undertake to adhere to IMCA's Code of Professional Conduct.

More information about each accredited consulting practice is available at **www.imca.ie**.

BearingPoint Ireland Limited
Montague House, Adelaide Road, Dublin 2
T: 01 418 1111 F: 01 418 1500
E: pat.moyne@bearingpoint.com W: www.bearingpoint.com
Formed: 2000
Contact: Pat Moyne

Fueled by the passion and capabilities of our more than 17,000 dedicated employees, BearingPoint helps solve clients' most pressing challenges day in and day out. From strategy to execution, our disciplined yet flexible approach starts and ends with you. We are BearingPoint, management and technology consultants.

Claritas Consulting
317 The Capel Building, St Mary's Abbey, Dublin 7
T: 01 828 0320 F: 01 828 0321
E: jdoyle@claritasconsulting.com W: www.claritasconsulting.com
Formed: 2004 Contact: James Doyle

We offer independent specialist advice and support to clients across a wide range of market sectors. We have well-proven and extensive experience in managing change through the key disciplines of business requirements analysis, business strategy development, business process analysis, design and change programme and project management.

Deloitte
Deloitte & Touche House, 29 Earlsfort Terrace, Dublin 2
T: 01 417 2200 F: 01 417 2300
E: dhearn@deloitte.ie W: www.deloitte.com/ie
Formed: 1845 Contact: David Hearn

Deloitte is Ireland's largest multi-disciplinary professional services firm. Our mission is to help our clients and our people excel. We are a member firm of Deloitte Touche Tohmatsu. Over 150 local consultants provide enterprise applications, technology, enterprise risk, outsourcing, strategy, operations, human capital, CFO and financial advisory services.

Farrell Grant Sparks (FGS)
Molyneux House, Bride Street, Dublin 8
T: 01 418 2000 F: 01 418 2050
E: fgs@fgs.ie W: www.fgs.ie
Formed: 1978 Contact: Tom Murray

FGS Consulting offers clients from the public, semi-State and private sectors a suite of advisory services, from strategic reviews and policy evaluation to feasibility studies and business planning. We have considerable experience and knowledge of strategic and operational issues that affect our clients' organizations.

Hay Group (Ireland) Limited
Newmount House, 22 - 24 Lower Mount Street, Dublin 2
T: 01 676 5994 F: 01 661 6623
E: haygroup_ireland@haygroup.com W: www.haygroup.ie
Formed: 1943 (globally), 1964 (Ireland) Contact: Des McDermott

Hay Group is a global human resources consulting firm, specialising in performance improvement through people. Our services include capability assessment, talent management, leadership transformation, organisation effectiveness, reward strategy, executive remuneration, reward information services, employee & customer surveys. We help human resource professionals, senior management and top teams to implement their strategies.

Prospectus Limited
Parkview House, Beech Hill, Clonskeagh, Dublin 14
T: 01 260 3122 F: 01 260 3130
E: strategy@prospectus.ie W: www.prospectus.ie
Formed: 1991 Contact: David W Duffy

Prospectus offers clients the full range of strategy services including: strategy development and implementation, M&A integration, governance and organization structures, sectoral reviews, business case development, market appraisals, and implementation planning. Prospectus works in financial services, food, healthcare, technology, the public sector, professional services, third-level institutions and the voluntary and community sectors.

REGISTERED CONSULTING PRACTICES

Registered Consulting Practices are consultancy organisations that are managed by Members or Fellows of IMCA who are Certified Management Consultants (CMC), and which undertake to adhere to IMCA's Code of Professional Conduct.

More information on each registered consulting practice is available at **www.imca.ie**.

A Carey & Associates Limited
36 Ballyglass, Ardnacrusha, Co Clare
T: 061 348 348 F: 061 348 349
E: info@careys.ie W: www.careys.ie
Formed: 2000 Contact: Alan Carey
Business analysis, business architecture, business planning, strategy formulation, change / transformation management, budgeting / financial planning services and accounting services.

Align Management Solutions
77 Beechwood Avenue Lower, Ranelagh, Dublin 6
T: 01 412 5890 F: 01 412 5899
E: mahern@alignmanagement.net W: www.alignmanagement.net
Formed 2002 Contact: Miriam P Ahern

Specialising in organisation development, management practice and employment relations. Includes: strategy; change management; staff development; performance management; team-working; mergers; best-practice HR policies; and compliance. Provided through consulting, facilitation, executive coaching and mentoring.

Barre Fitzpatrick & Associates
6 Rockville Drive, Blackrock, Co Dublin
T: 01 288 3078
E: barre@iol.ie
Formed: 1995 Contact: Barre Fitzpatrick

Strategy, innovation, facilitation, management development, management philosophy.

Brolyn Consultants Limited
73 St Helen's Road, Booterstown, Co Dublin
T: 01 210 9868 F: 01 210 9868
E: blynch@indigo.ie
Formed: 1987 Contact: Brendan Lynch

Feasibility studies, marketing plans, due diligence reports, EU funding, business planning and project finance. Also involved in manufacturing companies and technical start-ups. Serves both public and private sector.

Burnham House
40 Oak Dene, Killiney, Co. Dublin
T: 01 285 5588 F: 01 285 5588
E: brian@burnham.house.ie
Formed: 2002 Contact: Brian Barry

Public policy, corporate governance, strategic management, management reward.

Century Management
Century House, Newlands Business Park, Newlands Cross, Dublin 22
T: 01 459 5950 F: 01 459 5949
E: johnbutler@century management.ie W: www.centurymanagement.ie
Formed: 1989 Contact: John Butler

Century Management is primarily a strategy consultancy, engaged in human performance improvement, culminating in oprganisation-wide systemic and cultural change. Special focus areas include: leadership, succession planning, cultural transformation, competency management and business management.

Chaos Management

Carrigroe, Enniskeane, Bandon, Co Cork
T: 023 39956 F: 023 39956
E: paraic@ chaosmanagement.ie W: www.chaosmanagement.ie
Formed: 2007 Contact: Paraic Hegarty

Chaos Management specializes in helping clients to design and implement technology-enabled business strategies. This involves merger and acquisition IT due diligence, IT strategy development, programme and project management, specification and selection of systems / integrators and ongoing support for process re-design, change management and benefits / value realisation.

Chinook Consulting

Clermont, Blackrock, Dundalk, Co Louth
T: 042 932 1107   F: 042 932 1044
E: pjwarren@iol.ie
Formed: 2001 Contact: Padraig Warren

Independent evaluations of funded programmes, strategic management, mentoring, training and facilitation support to both public and private sectors. Development of quality management systems and business excellence. Assistance with strategy implementation and performance monitoring based on the Balanced Scorecard.

CHL Consulting Group

40 Northumberland Avenue, Dun Laoghaire, Co Dublin
T: 01 284 4760 F: 01 284 4775
E: mail@chl.ie W: www.chl.ie
Formed: 1984 Contact: Michael Counahan

Tourism, leisure, arts, cultural heritage, education and regional development. Services include strategic planning, project planning, marketing, economic analysis and planning.

Corporate Development
127 Mount Merrion Avenue, Blackrock, Co. Dublin
T: 087 256 6427 F: 01 2880697
E: dokeeffe@iol.ie
Formed: 2001 Contact: David O'Keeffe

Company turnaround, with expertise in business appraisal, business planning, organization and profit improvement programmes and solution implementation.

Cyril Kirwan & Associates
6 Maywood Park, Raheny, Dublin 3
T: 01 831 0469
E: ckirwan@indigo.ie
Formed: 1996

The company engages in two broad areas of activity: (1) Management development, including assessment, coaching and conducting learning and development events. (2) Design, evaluation and learning transfer of / from training and development activities.

Ennis & Co Business Consultants
McConnell Business Hall, Strandfield Business Park, Rosslare Road,
    Wexford
T: 053 918 4712 F: 053 918 4712
E: info@ennisco.ie W: www.ennisco.ie
Formed: 1993 Contact: Tony Ennis

Enterprise development assignments for clients, including State agencies and private industry. Areas of specialisation include: business strategic development, marketing, financial planning, international alliances, business plans, evaluation reports, special projects, management and business development training, mentoring / coaching and project work.

EPS Consulting Limited
5 Islington Avenue Mews, Sandycove, Co Dublin
T: 01 284 5528
E: pbrennan@epsconsult.ie W: www.epsconsult.ie
Formed: 2007

*EPS Consulting provides services in the fields of EU and Government affairs,
pubic procurement, economic and business research, public policy,
infrastructure planning, business strategy and advice on business
opportunities.*

European Telecommunications Management
44 Adelaide Road, Dublin 2
T: 01 676 7666
E: info@etm.ie W: www.etm.ie
Formed: 1986 Contact: Guy Johnston

*Designs and procures telecommunications solutions to meet the business needs
of organisations. These solutions cover the full spectrum of corporate needs,
including fixed and wireless communications, whether voice or data.*

FACIT Consulting Limited
Block 1, Blackrock Business Park, Blackrock, Co. Dublin
T: 01 288 4609 F: 01 283 3787
E: pat.nolan@facit.ie W: www.facit.ie
Formed: 1993 Contact: Pat Nolan

*IT business consulting, business continuity planning, facilities management,
programme management, project management, and technical / network support.*

Fitzpatrick Associates, Economic Consultants
122 Ranelagh Village, Dublin 6
T: 01 496 6008 F: 01 496 6028
E: info@fitzpatrick-associates.com W: www.fitzpatrick-associates.com
Formed: 1983 Contact: Jim Fitzpatrick

*Fitzpatrick Associates concentrate on economic and social analysis, public
policy analysis, project and programme evaluation.*

Galvia Management Consultants Limited
Church House, Main Street, Leixlip, Co Kildare
T: 01 458 1420 F: 01 458 1423
E: info@galviamc.com W: www.galviamc.com
Formed: 2003 Contacts: Michael Heneghan, Christopher Dunne

Sports facility construction and management, project management, strategic development and business development.

Hamilton & Co Management Consultants
28 South Frederick Street, Suite 150, Dublin 2
T: 01 677 8180 F: 01 677 6175
E: dr.hamilton@ireland.com
Formed: 1997 Contact: Brian Hamilton

Marketing and sales, interim general management, and strategy, with familiarity in two sectors: life insurance and film.

Hanley Consulting & Training
Seaview House, Rathlee, Easkey, Co. Sligo
T: 096 49950 F: 096 49950
E: seamus@hanleyct.com W: www.hanleyct.com
Formed: 1996 Contacts: Christopher Hanley, Seamus Hanley

Quality / safety consulting and training across all industrial sectors, ISO9001, HR and change management, HACCP in food / animal feed, 18001, Safe-T, safety management systems and statements, Safe Pass, train-the-trainer and manual handling.

International Human Resources Consultancy
Hemet, 48 Castleknock Park, Dublin 15
T: 01 826 2214 / 086 241 7518 F: 01 821 5121
E: gerrymc48@eircom.net W: www.ihrconsultancy.ie /
   www.twominds.ie
Formed: 1998 Contact: Gerry McLarnon

Providing a range of specialist HR services under five headings: (1) HR organisation, design and effectiveness. (2) Human resource development. (3)Facilitation processes, including coaching and mentoring. (4) Career evaluation and option appraisal. (5) Employee Assistance Programme (EAP) services. Also providing stress management and assertiveness training, both in-house and on an individual basis.

Invest-Tech Limited
27 Ardmeen Park, Blackrock, Co. Dublin
T: 01 283 4083 F: 01 278 2391
E: info@planware.org W: www.planware.org
Formed: 1978 Contact: Brian Flanagan

Business appraisals, strategy and planning, product and market research, financial planning, preparation of business plans, enterprise development, entrepreneurial training and venture initiation, development and sale of software packages for preparing financial projections and writing business plans.

Latitude
33 Coolkill, Sandyford, Dublin 18
T: 01 295 0688 F: 01 295 0877
E: lmcc@iol.ie
Formed: 1991 Contact: Lucy McCaffrey

Process consulting, focusing on change management, customer centricity and strategy development and implementation.

Linehan & Associates Consulting
34 Woodpark, Castleknock, Dublin 15
T: 086 608 6991 F: + 44 709 235 6679
E: lincar@indigo.ie
Formed: 2007 Contact: Billy Linehan

Business advisers and management consultants to innovative SMEs and organisations undergoing change. Particular strengths in strategic planning and subsequent implementation across business functions. Proven track record across a variety of sectors.

McIver Consulting
49 Upper Mount Street, Dublin 2
T: 01 676 6647 F: 01 661 2528
E: odonoghue@mc-iverconsulting.com
Formed: 1969 Contacts: Frank O'Donoghue, Con Gregg

Business strategy and planning, policy analysis., organisation development and general consultancy. Our policy work is in education, training, enterprise development and environmental management. We work in most sectors of Irish indigenous industry. We focus on food, tourism and retail.

MDR Consulting Limited
19 Elgin Road, Ballsbridge, Dublin 4
T: 01 634 9636 F: 01 281 5331
E: tommoriarty@mdrcl.com W: www.mdrcl.com
Formed: 2001 Contacts: Tom Moriarty

Performance improvement specialists with strengths in food and drink and healthcare sectors – accredited under HSE framework. Focus on major outsourcing, supply chain / plant rationalisation and merger / acquisition projects, as well as process capability / performance, overhead cost and working capital reduction. Also expertise in project management, sector reviews and programme evaluation.

O'Hurley Blair Irwin

3rd Floor, *Mountkennett House*, Henry Street, Limerick
T: 061 401122 F: 061 401144
E: cohurley@obi.ie W: www.obi.ie
Formed: 1994 Contact: Charlie O'Hurley

Corporate finance advice to high growth companies.

OLAS Software Training & Development

Maple House, Lower Kilmacud Road, Stilorgan, Co Dublin
T: 01 279 0020 F: 01 279 0029
E: monica.flood@olas.ie W: www.olas.ie
Formed: 1981 Contact: Monica Flood

Specialises in IT training and bespoke software development for corporates. Provides consulting on training needs analysis, training project management, training delivery support and post-training support. OLAS is SAP's Education Partner in Ireland. Also provides development services relating to databases, spreadsheets, automation and templates.

Options Consulting

Carrigard, Kilcoolishal, Glounthaune, Co. Cork
T: 021 435 1049 F: 021 435 5764
E: cynthia@optionsconsulting.ie W: www.optionsconsulting.ie
Formed: 2001 Contact: Cynthia Deane

Promoting strategic approaches to learning and development in all kinds of organisations, public and private sector. Management consultancy services targeted at education and training sectors, project planning, evaluation, monitoring and extensive EU experience.

P. V. O'Driscoll & Co Limited

3 Ashboro, Shanakiel, Cork
T: 02) 439 6884 F: 021 439 6884
E: pvodriscoll@eircom.net
Formed: 1985 Contact: Patrick V. O'Driscoll

Improving productivity and controlling unit labour costs in the FMCG logistics sector, using Industrial Engineering procedures.

Paul A Flynn & Associates
Anaverna, Ravensdale, Co Louth
T: 042 937 1654
E: flynnpa@indigo.ie
Formed: 1991 Contact: Paul Flynn

A firm of management consultants specialising in business development and training for growth and greater profitability. Specialist skills include: performance and financial management, evaluation, strategic management and transition implementation. Significant experience with large organisations, both public and private. Special interest in healthcare and start-ups.

Petrus Consulting Limited
Brookfield House, Carysfort Avenue, Blackrock, Co. Dublin
T: 01 283 3500 F: 01 280 0592
E: michael@petrusconsult.com W: www.petrusconsult.com
Formed: 1999 Contact: Michael Griffin

Petrus Consulting provides performance improvement solutions to public and private sector clients, using a process modelling and Balanced Scorecard approach. We also carry out expenditure reviews and value-for-money assessments. We review financial reporting systems and procedures and advise on regulatory reform issues, including impact analysis and de-regulation.

Platinum Consulting Group
Ulverton House, Ulverton Road, Dalkey, Co. Dublin
T: 01 235 2484 F: 01 235 2485
E: pcg@platinum.ie W: www.platinum.ie
Formed: 1994 Contact: Darragh B Murphy

Management strategies, marketing and business development strategies. Creative and innovative approaches to management development.

PRISM Management & Consulting Services
23 Fitzwilliam Square, Dublin 2
T: 01 676 2205 F: 01 661 9575
E: pcprism@indigo.ie
Formed: 1994 Contact: Philip Clarke

Getting regulatory approval, TPA outsourcing, controls and improvement, compliance and governance in the financial services sector.

Refraction Limited
5 The Village Centre, Clane, Co. Kildare
T: 045 982446 F: 045 861892
E: refraction@indigo.ie W: www.refraction.ie
Formed: 2003

Provides consultancy services in special care / childcare, health, public sector or voluntary sector, including: organisational reviews, strategic planning and change management, quality systems development and implementation and human resources management.

Riverwest Management Limited
128 The Park, Sallins Road, Naas, Co Kildare
T: 087 284 5760 F: 045 898504
E: jfitzsimons@rvrwst.com W: www.rvrwst.com
Formed: 2000 Contact: James Fitzsimons

We consult in several sectors and specialise in technology transfer between universities and companies, commercialisation of new technology, management of the research functions in small, medium and large companies and in intellectual property rights. We also research and exploit funding opportunities in R&D, rural development, marketing and training.

Strategic Computing Limited
Beckett House, 66 Clonkeen Drive, Foxrock, Dublin 18
T: 01 289 2522 F: 01 289 8321
E: murphyr@indigo.ie W: www.strategiccomputing.ie
Formed: 1986 Contact: Ray Murphy

Specialises in the area of software sourcing and procurement projects for large organisations. Development of sourcing strategies, management of major sourcing projects through RFI / RFP / ITT activities, provision of training courses and the development and customisation of sourcing methodologies and toolkits.

Talbot Associates Limited
33 Fitzwilliam Square, Dublin 2
T: 01 669 4704 F: 01 669 4794
E: patricktalbot@eircom.net W: www.talbotassociates.ie
Formed: 2002 Contact: Patrick Talbot

Project and programme evaluation, strategic and operational planning, organisation and process design, performance measurement and management.

Tom Martin & Associates / TMA
19 Priory Hall, Stillorgan, Co. Dublin
T: 01 283 5252 F: 01 283 5251
E: info@tma.ie W: www.tma.ie
Formed: 1988 Contact: Tom Martin

Services to public and private sectors relating to development, formulation and appraisal of human resource development, innovation, SME and service sector policies, feasibility studies, marketing and business planning.

Torc Consulting Group
4 Lower Pembroke Street, Dublin 2
T: 01 662 3020
E: info@torc.ie W: www.torc.ie
Formed: 1999 Contact: Patrick Collins

Management development: focusing on upskilling managers with the competencies required to run high-performance organisations, programmes are delivered through formal training and / or individual coaching. Change consulting and outplacement: we work with client companies to deliver organisational change strategies effectively, while keeping operations running smoothly. Management and executive recruitment: we provide a 'boutique' service to clients, using all methodologies, supported by research capacity and talent database to find the best executives, managers and key employees for our clients.

Tourism & Transport Consult International Limited
The Malt House, Grand Canal Quay, Dublin 2
T: 01 680 8833 F: 01 670 8731
E: info@ttc.ie W: www.ttc.ie
Formed: 1993 Contacts: Dermod Dwyer, Christopher Noel Sweeney

Tourism, transport, leisure, land use, policy development and policy analysis.

Waters Consulting Limited
Baltrasna, Ashbourne, Co. Meath
T: 01 835 2279 F: 01 835 7537
E: richard@waters.ie
Formed: 1991 Contact: Richard Waters

Helps companies develop financial, organisational and logistical answers that lead directly to marked transformations of financial and operational performance and profitability.

Willie H Maxwell & Associates
Europa Academy, Europa Campus, Balheary, Swords, Co Dublin
T: 01 883 9223 F: 01 813 8653
E: w.maxwell@ acumenprogramme.com
Formed: 2003 Contact: Willie Maxwell

Creation and delivery of economic development programmes within Ireland and Europe. Advising and assisting HPSU companies. Advising and assisting SMEs in growth and development phases.

WMJ Kelleher & Associates
Waterfront Business Centre, 5 Lapps Quay, Cork
T: 021 485 2929
E: wmjkelleher@eircom.net
Formed: 1995 Contact: Joseph Kelleher

Assistance in business evaluation and planning, feasibility studies, marketing plans, strategy development, financial planning and gaining ISO9000 and ISO14001 certification.

Yeaton & Associates Limited
19 Elgin Road, Ballsbridge, Dublin 4
T: 01 660 0500 F: 01 281 5331
E: info@yeatonassoc.com W: www.yeatonassoc.com
Formed: 2000 Contact: Tom Yeaton

Highly-professional executive search selection services that are based on candidate care, confidentiality and ongoing client relationships. Our assistance focuses on senior-level appointments and our approaches combine either research or advertising with intensive candidate evaluation, supplemented by psychometric assessment.

INDEPENDENT CONSULTANTS & ADVISERS GROUP

ICAG is a network of independent management consultants and also business advisers, who work within public and non-profit organisations. ICAG runs educational, networking, social and business-to-business events on an annual basis. A voluntary committee of its members (see below) manages the network.

ICAG is interested in engaging with other management consultants and business advisers and expanding its membership, which is open to any independent member of IMCA and members of small management consultancy houses that are members of the Institute. For further information, please contact the Chairperson on (01) 8203020 or at info@base-centre.com.

The ICAG Committee for 2007/08 is:

Kenneth Germaine (Chairperson)	BASE Enterprise Centre
Miriam Ahern (previous Chairperson)	Align Management Solutions
Patrick Nolan (Treasurer)	FACiT Consulting
Michael Rock	Act Now
Pamela Fay	Business Performance Perspectives Ltd
Krishna De	One Ocean Group
Ciaran Brady	PLS Plasma Logistics
Rex Coghlan	Visible Business Advice
Jim Fitzsimons	Riverwest Management Ltd.
Victor Brannigan	Enterprise Actions
Declan Byrne	Byrne Conroy Consulting

MEMBERS

Miriam Ahern (M / CMC)
Align Management Solutions
77 Beechwood Avenue Lower
Ranelagh
Dublin 6
T: 01 412 5890
F: 01 412 5890
E: mahern@alignmanagement.net

Breeta Allen (M / CMC)
Ryan Walsh & Associates
14 Clarinda Park North
Dun Laoghaire
Co Dublin
T: 086 601 5428
E: breeta@rwa.ie

Paul Allen (A)
Bearingpoint
Montague House
Adelaide Road
Dublin 2
T: 01 418 1105 / 086 179 1105
E: paul.allen@bearingpoint.com

Ross Allen (S)
Twyford
Baylin
Athlone
Co Westmeath
T: 09064 74930 / 086 354 5046
E: rosaldinio@gmail.com

Pedro Angulo (M / CMC)
Penna Consulting
9 Hanover Street East
Dublin 2
T: 01 673 1503
E: pedro.angulo@e-penna.com

Brian Arnold (A)
Agenda Consulting
Corduff Hall
Lusk
Co Dublin
T: 01 843 7356
E: brian.agendaconsulting@
    yahoo.ie

Zayneb Aziz (S)
12 Valley Drive
Druid Valley
Cabinteely
Dublin 18
T: 01 282 2664 / 087 971 7600
E: zayneb.aziz@gmail.com

F = Fellow; M = Member; A = Associate; S = Student; CMC = Certified Management Consultant

Ling Bai (A)
Baltrasna
Ashbourne
Co Meath
T: 01 658 1782 / 087 786 4227
E: bailing.bi@gmail.com

Frank Bannister (M / CMC)
Morehampton Consultancy
    Services
25 Morehampton Terrace
Donnybrook
Dublin 4
T: 01 896 2186
F: 01 667 0711
E: frank.bannister@tcd.ie

Tom Banville (M)
Wexford County Enterprise
    Board
Ardervan Business Park
Ardervan
Wexford
T: 053 22965
F: 053 24944
E: tom@wexfordceb.ie

Claire Barcoe (S)
29 St Annes Park
Shankill
Co Dublin
T: 01 282 0104 / 087 210 2127

Brian Barry (M / CMC)
Burnham House Limited
40 Oak Dene
Killiney
Co Dublin
T: 01 285 5588
F: 01 285 5588
E: brian@burnhamhouse.ie

Vincent Barton (M / CMC)
Prospectus Limited
Ashfield
Wynberg Park
Blackrock
Co Dublin
T: 01 218 0345
E: vbarton@prospectus.ie

Dearbhalla Baviera (A)
Deloitte
Deloitte & Touche House
29 Earlsfort Terrace
Dublin 2
T: 01 417 2200
F: 01 417 2300
E: dbaviera@deloitte.ie

Niall Baxter (A)
Bearingpoint
Montague House
Adelaide Road
Dublin 2
T: 01 418 1226
E: niall.baxter@bearingpoint.com

Robert Beggs (M)
Balbriggan Enterprise & Training
    Centre
Stephenstown Industrial Estate
Balbriggan
Co Dublin
T: 01 802 0401
F: 01 802 0455
E: rbeggs@beat.ie

Sinead Bent (S)
84 Goatstown Road
Goatstown
Dublin 14
T: 01 298 0662 / 086 399 2457

Adrian Blackshields (M / CMC)
Deloitte
City Quarter
Lapps Quay
Cork
T: 021 490 7034 / 087 930 1594
E: ablackshields@deloitte.ie

Cian Blackwell (A)
Grant Thornton
24-26 City Quay
Dublin 2
T: 01 680 5710 / 087 824 2652
E: cian.blackwell@
    grantthornton.ie

Alex Blayney (S)
27 Leeson Park
Dublin 6
T: 01 496 0101 / 087 784 0063
E: blayney007@hotmail.com

Patrick Boland (A)
Deloitte
Deloitte & Touche House
29 Earlsfort Terrace
Dublin 2
T: 01 417 2225 / 086 313 3790
F: 01 417 2300
E: pboland@deloitte.ie

Ian Booth (A)
Bearingpoint
Montague House
Adelaide Road
Dublin 2
T: 01 418 1186 / 086 179 1185
E: stephen.booth@
    bearingpoint.com

Michael Boyd (M / CMC)
Development Consultants
    International / DCI Limited
Ferry House
48 Lower Mount St
Dublin 2
T: 01 661 1903
F: 01 661 4991
E: michael.boyd@tdigroup.ie

Gerry Boyle (M / CMC)
FGS Partnership
Molyneux House
Bride Street
Dublin 8
T: 01 418 2000
E: dublin@fgspartnership.com

Stephen Boyle (M)
CSRM Limited
18 Shielmartin Road
Sutton
Dublin 13
T: 01 839 4893
F: 01 839 4893
E: sboyle@csrm.ie

Jim Bradley (M)
Catalysis Consulting Limited
Grianan
Cahercalla Road
Ennis
Co Clare
T: 087 2220300
E: catalysis@eircom.net

Michael Bradley (M)
Irish Franchise Association
Powderlough
Dunshaughlin
Co Meath
T: 01 825 9215
E: michaelbradley@ireland.com

Ciaran Brady (A)
Dalkey Business Club
17 Castle Street
Dalkey
Co Dublin
T: 086 853 4314 / 01 202 0020
E: ciaran@
    plsbusinesspartners.com

Victor Branagan (A)
Enterprise Actions
Ballyogan
Graig-na-Managh
Co Kilkenny
T: 059 972 5000 / 087 418 7082
F: 059 9725676
E: victor@enterpriseactions.ie

Anthony Breen (S)
8 Oaklawn
Ballyfin Road
Portlaoise
Co Laois
T: 0502 22640 / 087 693 7542
E: ajbreen@yahoo.com

Peter Brennan (M / CMC)
EPS Consulting
5 Islington Avenue Mews
Sandycove
Co Dublin
T: 01 284 5528 / 087 241 2001
E: pbrennan@epsconsult.ie

Sean Brennan (M)
Sean Brennan & Associates
Ballinasloe Enterprise &
    Technology Centre
Ballinasloe
Co Galway
T: 090 96 43083
E: sfbrennan@eircom.net

Blaise Brosnan (M)
Management Resource Institute
Glenanaar House
Hospital Road Park
Wexford
T: 053 9147774
E: blaise@mriwex.ie

Kenneth Buchholtz (A)
Cloncourt House
Ennistymon
Co Clare
T: 065 707 1933 / 086 809 2776
E: kenneth@
   campbellinternational.net

Conor Buckley (A)
Deloitte
City Quarter
Lapps Quay
Cork
T: 01 417 2487 / 087 772 9960
E: cobuckley@deloitte.ie

Fred Buckley (A)
Burnham Consulting
Lough Dan Road
Roundwood
Co Wicklow
T: 086 103 3250
E: fbuckley@burnham.ie

John Buckley (F)
Momentum Business Coaching
Clark House
Naas
Co Kildare
T: 045 881888
F: 045 881999
E: jbuckley@momentumcoach.ie

Katie Burke (M / CMC)
Prospectus Limited
3 Greenville Parade
Blackpitts
Dublin 8
T: 01 218 0308
E: kburke@prospectus.ie

Michael Burke (S)
20 Irishtown Road
Dublin 4
T: 086 3552131
E: michaelburke83@gmail.com

Noel Burke (A)
NB Property Developments
   Limited
155 Upper Salthill
Galway
T: 091 502780
F: 091 502798
E: noel.burke@nbd.ie

Imelda K Butler (M / CMC)
Century Management Limited
Century House
Newlands Business Park
Newlands Cross
Dublin 22
T: 01 459 5950
F: 01 459 5949
E: imeldabutler@
   centurymanagement.ie

F = Fellow; M = Member; A = Associate; S = Student; CMC = Certified Management Consultant

John Butler (F / CMC)
Century Management Limited
Century House
Newlands Business Park
Newlands Cross
Dublin 22
T: 01 459 5950
F: 01 459 5949
E: johnbutler@
	centurymanagement.ie

Dermot Butterfield (A)
Bearingpoint
Montague House
Adelaide Road
Dublin 2
T: 087 241 1553
E: dermot.butterfield@
	bearingpoint.com

Aidan Byrne (A)
Blackstairs Technologies Limited
Rathvarrin
Ardattin
Carlow
T: 059 9155550
E: abyrne@blackstairs.ie

David Byrne (S)
Ardlaun House
Hayestown
Navan
Co Meath
T: 085 714 9747 / 046 902 4805
E: davyb2000@hotmail.com

Declan Byrne (A)
Byrne Conroy Consulting
Terenure Enterprise Centre
17 Rathfarnham Road
Terenure
Dublin 6W
T: 01 490 3238 / 086 822 5628
E: dbyrne@byrneconroy.ie

Louise Byrne (S)
18 Gleann Na Smol
Blackrock
Co Dublin
T: 01 280 3054 / 086 602 2198
E: louise_byrne2003@yahoo.co.uk

Pat Byrne (A)
Bearingpoint
Montague House
Adelaide Road
Dublin 2
T: 01 418 1111 / 086 837 6414
E: pat.byrne@bearingpoint.com

Eamonn Caffrey (S)
9 Priory Chase
St Raphael's Manor
Celbridge
Co Kildare
T: 01 610 2914 / 086 856 3906
E: eamonncaffrey@eircom.net

Maria Caldwell (M / CMC)
Farrell Grant Sparks
Molyneux House
Bride Street
Dublin 9
T: 01 418 2039
E: mcaldwell@fgs.ie

John Callan (S)
The Warren
Boyle
Co Roscommon
T: 071 966 2092 / 086 804 2766
E: johngcallan@yahoo.ie

Maria Callinan (M)
Laois County Enterprise Board
Portlaoise Enterprise Centre
Clonminan Business Park
Portlaoise
Co Laois
T: 057 86 61800
F: 057 86 61797
E: maria@laoisenterprise.com

David Canning (A)
Bearingpoint
Montague House
Adelaide Road
Dublin 2
T: 01 820 1743 / 087 247 7098
E: david.canning@
    bearingpoint.com

Michael Cantwell (A)
Limerick County Council
Garnafana
Toomevara
Nenagh
Co Tipperary
T: 061 319319 / 087 810 8649
E: mike@lcoeb.ie

Alan Carey (M / CMC)
Carey & Assoociates
7 Sheelin Road
Caherdavin Park
Limerick
T: 061 325600 / 087 667 5110
F: 061 325602
E: alan.carey@careys.ie

Alice Carroll (A)
Deloitte
Deloitte & Touche House
29 Earlsfort Terrace
Dublin 2
T: 01 417 2813
F: 01 417 2300
E: acarroll@deloitte.ie

Niall Carroll (F)
ACT Venture Capital Limited
6 Richview Office Park
Clonskeagh
Dublin 14
T: 01 260 0966
F: 01 260 0538
E: ncarroll@actvc.ie

Kenneth Carroll (A)
Carroll Food Services Limited
4 Thorn Castle Street
Dublin 4
T: 01 668 6095
F: 01 660 0035
E: kcarroll@
    carrollfoodservices.com

F = Fellow; M = Member; A = Associate; S = Student; CMC = Certified Management Consultant

Eimear Maria Casey (A)
Deloitte
Deloitte & Touche House
29 Earlsfort Terrace
Dublin 2
T: 01 417 2262 / 086 846 5312
F: 01 417 2300
E: ecasey@deloitte.ie

John Casey (M)
9 Upper Carysfort Avenue
Blackrock
Co Dublin
T: 086 194 1408
E: interimresources@eircom.net

Tadhg Cashman (M / CMC)
Morse
83 Woodford
Stillorgan
Co Dublin
T: 01 292 1438
E: tadhg.cashman@morse.ie

Paul Caskey (A)
41B Carysfort Avenue
Blackrock
Co Dublin
T: 086 824 5150
E: paulcaskey@hotmail.com

David Cass (M / CMC)
Deloitte
Deloitte & Touche House
29 Earlsfort Terrace
Dublin 2
T: 01 417 2629 (W) / 01 269 7510 /
    087 829 2628
F: 01 417 2300
E: dcass@deloitte.ie

Declan Cassidy (M / CMC)
Deloitte
Barnaderg
Tuam
Co Galway
T: 01 417 2887
E: declan.cassidy@deloitte.ie

Louise Church (A)
OlasIT - Software Training &
    Development
Maple House
Lower Kilmacud Road
Stillorgan
Co Dublin
T: 01 279 0020
F: 01 279 0029
E: louise.church@olas.ie

Niall Clarke (A)
Bearingpoint
Montague House
Adelaide Road
Dublin 2
T: 01 418 1264 / 086 837 2428
E: niall.clarke@bearingpoint.com

Philip Clarke (M / CMC)
Prism Management & Consulting
    Services
23 Fitzwilliam Square
Dublin 2
T: 01 676 2205
F: 01 6619 575
E: pcprism@indigo.ie

Anne-Marie Codd (A)
CORI
Presentation Sisters
27 Abbeyfield
Kilcock
Co Kildare
T: 01 505 3000 (W) / 01 628 4579 /
    086 848 4733
F: 01 6689460
E: coddanne@eircom.net

Fergal Coffey (A)
Bearingpoint
Montague House
Adelaide Road
Dublin 2
T: 086 827 2611
E: fergal.coffey@
    bearingpoint.com

Rex Coghlan (M)
Visible Business Advice
Emerald House
Bluebell Industrial Estate
Bluebell
Dublin 12
T: 01 496 7492
F: 01 409 7833
E: visible@eircom.net

Ruth Colgan (M / CMC)
Deloitte
Deloitte & Touche House
29 Earlsfort Terrace
Dublin 2
T: 01 417 2871 / 086 818 5473
F: 01 417 2300
E: rcolgan@deloitte.ie

Gerard Collins (M)
Collane Consultants & Associates
89 Main Street
Cavan
T: 049 437 1500
F: 049 437 1502
E: collane@iol.ie

Jeffrey Collins (S)
14 Nutley Lane
Donnybrook
Dublin 4
T: 01 269 2306 / 086 830 1425
E: gully91@hotmail.com

Patrick Collins (M / CMC)
Torc Consulting Group
4 Lower Pembroke Street
Dublin 2
T: 01 662 3020/1
F: 01 662 3022
E: pc@torc.ie

Una Condron (S)
158 Roebuck Castle
Clonskeagh
Dublin 14
T: 01 288 6615 / 086 304 8714
E: unacondron@hotmail.com

Alan Conlan (M / CMC)
Conlan Technology Limited /
    Alan P Conlan & Associates
23 Lower Ormond Quay
Dublin 1
T: 01 872 9377
F: 01 872 9376
E: info@conlan.ie

Nicola Connolly (A)
24 Dornden Park
Booterstown
Co Dublin
T: +59 352 529 121 / 01 283 8977
E: niki_connolly@yahoo.com

Craig Conway (A)
Bearingpoint
Montague House
Adelaide Road
Dublin 2
T: 087 232 1446 / 01 418 1115
E: craig.conway@
   bearingpoint.com

Thomas Cooney (M)
Grow Your Business
Greenmount
Castlebellingham
Co Louth
T: 087 294 0812
E: info@gyb.ie

Cathy Cooper (S)
28 Beechwood Lawns
Rathcoole
Co Dublin
T: 01 458 8137 / 087 243 4469
E: cathycooper@gmail.com

Anthony Corrigan (S)
104 Marian Park
Drogheda
Co Louth
T: 087 796 0674
E: anthony.corrigan.2@
   student.ucd.ie

Georgina Corscadden (M / CMC)
108 Foxrock Park
Foxrock
Dublin 18
T: 01 289 8009 / 087 239 4544
E: georginacorscadden@
   eircom.net

Philippe Cosson (A)
Fitzwilliam Hall
27 Fitzwilliam Place
Dublin 2
T: 01 669 4648 / 087 207 8071
E: pcosson@ap-partners.com

Jillian Cotter (A)
Deloitte
Deloitte & Touche House
29 Earlsfort Terrace
Dublin 2
T: 01 417 2631 / 086 806 0760
F: 01 417 2300
E: jcotter@deloitte.ie

Liam Cotter (A)
Bearingpoint
Montague House
Adelaide Road
Dublin 2
T: 01 418 1117 / 086 179 1117
E: liam.cotter@bearingpoint.com

Michael Counahan (F / CMC)
CHL Consulting Group
40 Northumberland Avenue
Dun Laoghaire
Co Dublin
T: 01 284 4760
F: 01 284 4775
E: mcounahan@chl.ie

F = Fellow; M = Member; A = Associate; S = Student; CMC = Certified Management Consultant

Nicola Cox (A)
Bearingpoint
Montague House
Adelaide Road
Dublin 2
T: 086 179 1160
E: nicola.cox@bearingpoint.com

John Crawley (A)
Crawley Business Consulting
24 Main Street
Blackrock
Co Dublin
T: 01 211 0781
F: 01 211 0781
E: cbc@johncrawley.com

Sinead Crowley (S)
Cloonlara
Rathanker
Monkstown
Co Dublin
T: 021 484 1532 / 086 173 1270
E: crowleysinead@hotmail.com

Ronan Crummy (A)
Farrell Grant Sparks
Molyneux House
Bride Street
Dublin 8
T: 01 418 2000 / 087 803 4819
E: rcrummy@fgs.ie

Bertie Cuffe (A)
Cuffe & Company (Insurance)
Limited
10 Kings Terrace
Lower Glanmire Road
Cork
T: 021 450 0642 / 086 855 8989
E: bertie@cuffeco.ie

Zheng Cui (A)
Bearingpoint
Montague House
Adelaide Road
Dublin 2
T: 087 754 7984
E: zheng.cui@bearingpoint.com

Thomas Cullen (A)
Thomas Cullen & Associates /
Abacus Business Coaching
Unit 1, Liffey Valley Downs
Liffey Valley Park
Lucan
Co Dublin
T: 01 610 8468 / 085 738 5323
F: 01 610 8468
E: abacusbusinesscoaching@
msn.com

Liam Cusack (M)
Clonlough
Mitchelstown
Co Cork
T: 025 84918
F: 025 84169
E: cusackliam@eircom.net

Sarah Dallaghan (M)
97 Fairways
Rathfarnham
Dublin 14
T: 01 493 3243
E: sarah@hi-sales.com

Elaine Daly (M / CMC)
Farrell Grant Sparks
Molyneux House
Bride Street
Dublin 8
T: 01 418 2070
E: edaly@fgs.ie

Patrick D'Arcy (M)
4 Sugarloaf Peaks
Kilmacanogue
Co Wicklow
T: 01 286 6825
F: 01 286 6825
E: patrickjdarcy@eircom.net

Paul Davis (A)
Davis Business Consultants
Minley House
Newtownpark Avenue
Blackrock
Co Dublin
T: 01 288 5563 / 086 810 8548
E: paul@davisbc.com

Xavier de Bustos (S)
Nathema Limited
Embassy House
Herbert Park Lane
Dublin 4
T: 01 667 3812 / 087 799 3520
E: xdb@nathema.com

Edward De Groot (M / CMC)
De Groot Systems Limited
3A Woodlands Park
Mount Merrion Avenue
Blackrock
Co Dublin
T: 01 288 0170
F: 01 278 7010
E: edegroot@gofree.indigo.ie

Cynthia Deane (M / CMC)
Options Consulting
Carrigard
Kilcoolishal
Glounthane
Co Cork
T: 021 435 1049 / 087 241 3615
E: cynthia@optionsconsulting.ie

Ailish Delaney (S)
Main Street
Johnstown
Co Kilkenny
T: 056 883 1434 / 087 794 6421
E: ailish.delaney@ucdconnect.ie

Patrick Delaney (M / CMC)
Ovation Group
1 Clarinda Park North
Dun Laoghaire
Co Dublin
T: 01 280 2641
F: 01 280 5405
E: pdelaney@ovation.ie

F = Fellow; M = Member; A = Associate; S = Student; CMC = Certified Management Consultant

Assunta Delany (F)
FÁS
57/60 Jervis Street
Dublin 1
T: 01 804 4634
F: 01 804 4634
E: assunta.delany@fas.ie

Edward Delany (M / CMC)
Edward Delany & Associates
Woodtown
Drumree
Co Meath
T: 01 825 9757
F: 01 825 0693
E: eddelany@iol.ie

Anne-Marie Derham (A)
Bearingpoint
Montague House
Adelaide Road
Dublin 2
T: 086 179 1184 / 01 418 1184
E: anne-marie.derham@
      bearingpoint.com

Kieran Devery (M / CMC)
Deloitte
Deloitte & Touche House
29 Earlsfort Terrace
Dublin 2
T: 01 417 2532
F: 01 417 2300
E: kdevery@deloitte.ie

Diamond Ebs (A)
Diamond Business Academy
2 Mourne Place
Skerries
Co Dublin
T: 01 440 7491 / 085 733 1067
F: 01 810 6012
E: diamondebs@dbacademy.ie

Alan Dilleen (A)
18 Linenhall Terrace
Dublin 7
T: 01 828 0321 / 087 202 8098
E: adilleen@
      claritasconsulting.com

Jarlath Doherty (M / CMC)
Deloitte
Deloitte & Touche House
29 Earlsfort Terrace
Dublin 2
T: 01 417 2949 / 086 824 3727
F: 01 417 2300

Kevin Dooley (M / CMC)
Deloitte
11 Riverview
Scarriff
Co Clare
T: 061 921448
E: kedooley@deloitte.ie

Rosaleen Doonan (A)
Summerville Healthcare
Tataoibhe
Shannon
Co Sligo
T: 071 912 8430 / 071 914 5440 /
      087 419 0342
E: rdoonan1@eircom.net

F = Fellow; M = Member; A = Associate; S = Student; CMC = Certified Management Consultant

Michelle Dowling (A)
Bearingpoint
Montague House
Adelaide Road
Dublin 2
T: 086 179 2000 / 01 418 1127
E: michelle.dowling@
      bearingpoint.com

Michael Downes (M / CMC)
Deloitte
98 Trimleston Gardens
Booterstown
Co Dublin
T: 01 4172591 (W) / 01 260 3421 /
      087 266 9756
E: michael.downes@deloitte.ie

Ciara Susan Doyle (A)
Deloitte
Deloitte & Touche House
29 Earlsfort Terrace
Dublin 2
T: 01 417 2200 / 086 384 6016
F: 01 417 2300
E: cidoyle@deloitte.ie

James Doyle (A)
28 Glenbrook Park
Rathfarnham
Dublin 14
T: 01 828 0321 / 087 272 8164
E: jdoyle@claritasconsulting.com

Keira Doyle (S)
38 Castleknock Avenue
Laurel Lodge
Dublin 15
T: 01 821 7321 / 086 885 0934
E: keiradoyle@hotmail.com

Maura Doyle (A)
Kiltealy Associates Limited
91 Sandymount Avenue
Dublin 4
T: 01 269 7394
E: doylemaura@eircom.net

Yvonne Doyle (A)
Bearingpoint
Montague House
Adelaide Road
Dublin 2
T: 086 179 1230
E: yvonne.doyle@
      bearingpoint.com

Etain Doyle (M / CMC)
Linden
4 York Avenue
Rathmines
Dublin 6
T: 01 804 9600 / 086 244 8526
E: doyleetain@hotmail.com

Gerard Doyle (M / CMC)
Creative Change Limited
5 College Way
Clane
Co Kildare
T: 045 902790 / 086 190 2000
E: info@creative-change-
      ireland.com

Anne Duffy (A)
Neilstown
Bohermeen
Navan
Co Meath
T: 046 907 0033 / 087 908 7808
E: annetduffy@eircom.net

F = Fellow; M = Member; A = Associate; S = Student; CMC = Certified Management Consultant

David Duffy (M / CMC)
Prospectus Limited
Parkview House
Beech Hill
Clonskeagh
Dublin 4
T: 01 260 3122
F: 01 260 3130
E: dduffy@prospectus.ie

Mike Duignan (A)
MDR Management Services
19 Elgin Road
Ballsbridge
Dublin 4
T: 045 874651 / 086 242 3779
E: mikeduignan@mdr.ie

Grace Dunne (S)
15 Monastery Gate Green
Monastery Gate
Monastery Road
Clondalkin
Dublin 22
T: 01 459 5759 / 086 849 6899
E: grace_dunne@esatclear.ie

Aoidhbhin Durkin (A)
Bearingpoint
Montague House
Adelaide Road
Dublin 2
T: 087 672 0550
E: aoidhbhin.durkin@
    bearingpoint.com

Dermod Dwyer (M / CMC)
Tourism & Transport Consult
    International Limited
The Malt House
Grand Canal Quay
Dublin 2
T: 01 670 8833
F: 01 670 8731
E: dwyer@iol.ie

Tony Ennis (M / CMC)
Ennis & Co (Business
    Consultants)
McConnell Business Hall
Strandfield Business Park
Rosslare Road
Wexford
T: 053 9184712
F: 053 9184712
E: info@ennisco.ie

Chukwuma Obinna Ezebuiro (S)
142 Harcourt Green
Charlemont Street
Dublin 2
T: 01 478 4676 / 087 783 0211
E: ezebuiro@campus.ie

Pat Fahy (M)
Creg Marketing & Management
    Consultants Limited
Cregmore
Claregalway
Co Galway
T: 091 798117
F: 091 798439
E: cregass@eircom.net

Bernard Faughey (A)
Quinn School of Business / BJF
    Consulting
146 Sandyford Road
Dundrum
Dublin 16
T: 01 294 4003
F: 01 294 4003
E: bernardf@bjfconsulting.com

Pamela Fay (A)
Business Performance
    Perspectives Limited
70 Glenmalure Square
Milltown
Dublin 6
T: 01 260 6528 / 086 173 7125
E: pamela@bpp.ie

Ciara Finlay (S)
The Quarries
Airagar
Mountmellick
Co Laois
T: 057 862 4408 / 087 478 4452
E: ciarafinlay5@hotmail.com

Brian Finnegan (S)
6 Ardagh Court
Blackrock
Co Dublin
T: 01 278 1840 / 087 665 5877
E: brian.finnegan@ucdconnect.ie

Gerard Fitzgerald (A)
Bearingpoint
Montague House
Adelaide Road
Dublin 2
T: 086 179 1131 / 01 418 1131
E: gerard.fitzgerald@
    bearingpoint.com

John Fitzgerald (M / CMC)
John Fitzgerald & Associates
6 Sullivan's Quay
Cork
T: 021 496 3877
F: 021 431 0273
E: fitassoc@iol.ie

Sinead Fitzgerald (A)
11 Wolseley Street
South Circular Road
Dublin 8
T: 01 828 0321 / 087 285 4840
E: sfitzgerald@
    claritasconsulting.com

Stuart Fitzgerald (A)
Fitzgerald Power Chartered
    Accountants
Greyfriars
Waterford
T: 051 870152 / 086 344 1738
E: sfitzgerald@fitzgeraldpower.ie

Barre Fitzpatrick (M / CMC)
6 Rockville Drive
Blackrock
Co Dublin
T: 01 288 3078
E: barre@iol.ie

F = Fellow; M = Member; A = Associate; S = Student; CMC = Certified Management Consultant

Jim Fitzpatrick (M / CMC)
Fitzpatrick Associates, Economic
    Consultants
122 Ranelagh Village
Dublin 6
T: 01 496 6008
F: 01 496 6028
E: info@fitzpatrick-associates.com

James Fitzsimons (M / CMC)
Riverwest Management
128 The Park
Sallins Road
Naas
Co Kildare
T: 087 2845760
F I: 045 898504
E: jfitzsimons@rvrwst.com

Alan Flanagan (M / CMC)
Deloitte
Deloitte & Touche House
29 Earlsfort Terrace
Dublin 2
T: 01 417 2873
F: 01 417 2300
E: alan.flanagan@deloitte.ie

Brian Flanagan (F / CMC)
Invest-Tech Limited
27 Ardmeen Park
Blackrock
Co Dublin
T: 01 283 4083
F: 01 278 2391
E: brian@planware.org

Monica Flood (M / CMC)
OlasIT Software Training &
    Development Limited
Maple House
Lower Kilmacud Road
Stilorgan
Co Dublin
T: 01 279 0020
F: 01 279 0029
E: monica.flood@olas.ie

Charles Flynn (A)
Flynn & Associates Registered
    Auditors
Station Road
Dunboyne
Co Meath
T: 01 810 6819 / 087 687 4751
E: tflynn6@hotmail.com

Conail Flynn (A)
Grant Thornton Financial
    Counselling Limited
24/26 City Quay
Dublin 2
T: 01 680 5805
F: 01 680 5806
E: cflynn@gt-irl.com

Dean Flynn (A)
Deloitte
Deloitte & Touche House
29 Earlsfort Terrace
Dublin 2
T: 01 4178507
F: 01 417 2300
E: dflynn@deloitte.ie

F = Fellow; M = Member; A = Associate; S = Student; CMC = Certified Management Consultant

Patrick Flynn (A)
Bearingpoint
Montague House
Adelaide Road
Dublin 2
T: 01 418 1111 / 086 827 2596
E: patrick.flynn@
    bearingpoint.com

Paul Flynn (M / CMC)
Paul A Flynn & Associates
Anaverna Cottage
Ravensdale
Dundalk
Co Louth
T: 042 937 1654 / 086 166 2933
E: flynnpa@indigo.ie

John Foley (A)
eTEC Consulting Services
Effernock Manor
Dublin Road
Trim
Co Meath
T: 046 943 8920 / 086 813 2006
E: john_foley@etec.ie

Desmond Frazer (F / CMC)
Management Consultant
    Partners & Associates
33 Fitzwilliam Square
Dublin 2
T: 01 676 1802
F: 01 676 1803
E: dfrazer@iol.ie

Orla Gallagher (A)
6 Goldsmith Hall
Collegewood
Castleknock
Dublin 15
T: 01 828 0321 / 087 988 8124
E: ogallagher@
    claritasconsulting.com

Ronan Gallagher (S)
25 Dextar Terrace
Northbrook Road
Ranelagh
Dublin 6
T: 01 496 0544 / 087 759 4675
E: rjgallagher@hotmail.com

Brian Gartlan (M / CMC)
Deloitte
Drumgeeny
Corcreaghy
Carrickmacross
Co Monaghan
T: 01 417 2847
E: brian.gartlan@deloitte.ie

Kenneth Germaine (M)
BASE Enterprise Centre
Ladyswell Road
Mulhuddart
Dublin 15
T: 01 820 3020
F: 01 820 9469
E: ken.germaine@base-centre.com

Mark Gilleece (A)
Bearingpoint
Montague House
Adelaide Road
Dublin 2
T: 086 179 1106 / 01 418 1106
E: mgilleece@gmail.com

Avril Gleeson (A)
Bearingpoint
Montague House
Adelaide Road
Dublin 2
T: 086 179 2002 / 01 418 1144
E: avril.gleeson@
     bearingpoint.com

Yvonne Gleeson (S)
170 Ballygall Road East
Glasnevin
Dublin 11
T: 01 834 1655 / 086 845 6616
E: evg@02.ie

Billy Glennon (M / CMC)
Vision Consulting Group
East Point
Fairview
Dublin 3
T: 01 240 0200
F: 01 240 0 201
E: bglennon@vision.com

Sabrina Glynn (A)
Deloitte
Deloitte & Touche House
29 Earlsfort Terrace
Dublin 2
T: 01 417 2330 / 086 100 5742
F: 01 417 2300
E: sglynn@deloitte.ie

Niamh Gordon (S)
14 Beechpark Lawn
Castleknock
Dublin 15
T: 01 820 5114 / 085 733 4365
E: niamh.gordon@ucdconnect.ie

Wesley Gorman (A)
Bearingpoint
Montague House
Adelaide Road
Dublin 2
T: 087 698 2632
E: wesley.gorman@gmail.com

Paul Goubran (S)
5 Mervyn Court
Croswaithe Park
Dun Laoghaire
Co Dublin
T: 01 230 0656 / 087 690 0916
E: goubran_70@hotmail.com

Claire Goulding (M / CMC)
Deloitte
Deloitte & Touche House
29 Earlsfort Terrace
Dublin 2
T: 01 417 2484 / 087 123 3079
F: 01 417 2300

Stephen Graham (A)
346 Morell Avenue
Naas
Co Dublin
T: 01 828 0321 / 086 351 2404
E: sgraham@
     claritasconsulting.com

Kwame Gravenir (S)
Carnoomore Lodge
Clostoken
Loughrea
Co Galway
T: 086 8774279
E: kwame.gravenir@
     ucd.connect.ie

Sarah Gray (S)
43 Highfield Road
Rathgar
Dublin 6
T: 01 491 1066 / 087 661 1367
E: sarahgray2003@yahoo.com

Con Gregg (M / CMC)
Publica Consulting
49 Upper Mount Street
Dublin 2
T: 01 676 6647
F: 01 661 2528
E: con.gregg@publica.ie

Michael Griffin (F / CMC)
Petrus Consulting Limited
Brookfield House
Carysfort Avenue
Blackrock
Co Dublin
T: 01 288 7060 / 086 245 3452
F: 01 288 7060
E: michael@petrusconsult.com

Tom Grimes (F / CMC)
Talbot Associates
66 Windsor Drive
Monkstown
Co Dublin
T: 01 669 4704
F: 01 669 4794
E: thomasgrimes@eircom.net

Y Miao Guo (S)
Room 139, Blackrock Residence
Michael Smurfit School of
     Business
UCD
Belfield
Dublin 4
T: 086 868 8232
E: cecily999@yahoo.com

Patrick Gurren (A)
HR Consultant
12 Coleville Avenue
Clonmel
Co Tipperary
T: 087 983 3572
E: pat@gurren.ie

Brian Hamilton (A)
Hamilton & Associates
Suite 150
28 South Frederick Street
Dublin 2
T: 01 677 8180 / 087 290 2053
F: 01 677 6175
E: dr.hamilton@ireland.com

Roy Hanan (Hon. F)
Adaptech Consulting Limited
5 Highfield Court
Marley Grange
Dublin 16
T: 01 494 4396 (W) / 01 4944372 /
    087 232 4452
E: roy_hanan@yahoo.co.uk

Christopher Hanley (M / CMC)
Hanley Consulting & Training
Seaview House
Rathlee
Easkey
Co Sligo
T: 087 230 5121 / 096 49950
E: seamus@hanleyct.com

Conor Hanlon (M / CMC)
Deloitte
Deloitte & Touche House
29 Earlsfort Terrace
Dublin 2
T: 01 417 2836
F: 01 417 2300
E: conor.hanlon@deloitte.ie

Michael Hanna (M)
Performance Enhancement
Corrstown Road
Upper Ballinderry
Antrim BT28 2NH
Northern Ireland
T: 0044 28 9265 0411
E: michael@pesolutions.co.uk

Olwyn Hanrahan (M / CMC)
Deloitte
Deloitte & Touche House
29 Earlsfort Terrace
Dublin 2
T: 01 417 2200
F: 01 417 2300
E: ohanrahan@deloitte.ie

Gearoid Hardy (A)
GPH Consulting Limited
9 Sycamore Lawn
The Park
Cabinteely
Dublin 18
T: 087 249 9615 / 01 285 0794
E: ghardy@iol.ie

Audrey Harkin (M / CMC)
Deloitte
Deloitte & Touche House
29 Earlsfort Terrace
Dublin 2
T: 01 417 2823
F: 01 417 2300
E: audrey.harkin@deloitte.ie

Ronnie Harkin (A)
TDI Group
118 Clifden Court
Ellis Quay
Dublin 7
T: 01 677 9933 / 086 821 0969
E: ronnieharkin@eircom.net

Michael Hayden (M)
Dun Laoghaire-Rathdown
    County Enterprise Board
Nutgrove Enterprise Park
Nutgrove Way
Rathfarnham
Dublin 14
T: 01 494 8400
F: 01 494 8410
E: michael.hayden@dlrceb.ie

Grainne Healy (M / CMC)
Deloitte
Deloitte & Touche House
29 Earlsfort Terrace
Dublin 2
T: 01 417 2200 / 087 838 8119
F: 01 417 2300
E: grhealy@deloitte.ie

Peter Healy (A)
Deloitte
The Pines
Tullanisky
Mullingar
Co Westmeath
T: 01 417 2849 / 087 763 9473
E: phealy@deloitte.ie

David Hearn (M / CMC)
Deloitte
Deloitte & Touche House
29 Earlsfort Terrace
Dublin 2
T: 01 417 2535
F: 01 417 2300
E: david.hearne@deloitte.ie

Niamh Heavin (S)
Ribstown
Batterstown
Dunboyne
Co Meath
T: 01 825 9049 / 087 636 8166
E: niamh.heavin2@mail.dcu.ie

Maria Hegarty (M / CMC)
Equality Strategies Limited
491 Pearse Villas
Sallynoggin
Co Dublin
T: 087 230 4820
F: 01 679 5013
E: mariahegarty@
    equalitystrategies.ie

Paraic Hegarty (M / CMC)
Chaos Management
Carrigroe
Enniskeane
Bandon
Co Cork
T: 023 39956
F: 023 39956
E: paraic@ chaosmanagement.ie
W: www.chaosmanagement.ie

Michael Heneghan (A)
Galvia Management Consultants
Church House
Main Street
Leixlip
Co Kildare
T: 01 4581420
F: 01 45814233
E: michael@galviamc.com

Suzanne Hennessy (A)
Bearingpoint
Montague House
Adelaide Road
Dublin 2
T: 086 179 1148 / 01 418 1148
E: suzanne.hennessy@
    bearingpoint.com

Michele Henry (A)
11 Camden Street, Upper Flat 2
Dublin 2
T: 01 496 5303 / 086 813 9331
E: michele.henry@yahoo.com

Michael Hensey (A)
Hensey Consulting & Associates
9 Haddington Square
Beggars Bush
Dublin 4
T: 087 682 1390
E: henseyconsulting@eircom.net

Stephen Hilliard (S)
140 Shanganagh Cliffs
Shankill
Co Dublin
T: 087 968 7069
E: stephenhilliard2@hotmail.com

Andra Hodgson (S)
Apt 21, *Turnstone*
Thornwood
Booterstown
Blackrock
Co Dublin
T: 086 1721806
E: hodgson.andra@gmail.com

Brid Horan (F)
ESB
13 Oak Glade
Craddockstown
Naas
Co Kildare
T: 01 702 7380
F: 01 638 8025
E: brid.horan@mail.esb.ie

Kieran Horgan (A)
Maybridge Business Consulting
    Limited
Stone House
Main Street
Celbridge
Co Kildare
T: 01 610 2570 / 086 298 7004
F: 01 6303049
E: maybridgeconsultants@
    eircom.net

Victoria Hosking (A)
Prospectus Limited
73e Bellevue Apartments
Islandbridge
Dublin 8
T: 01 218 0320
E: vhosking@prospectus.ie

Cathal Houlihan (S)
Apartment G02-02
Glenomena Residences
UCD Belfield
Dublin 4
T: 087 654 8917
E: cathal.houlihan.2@
    student.ucd.ie

Desmond Howett (A)
Howett Consulting
10 Offington Court
Sutton
Dublin 13
T: 01 839 3393 (W) / 01 839 1722 /
    01 839 0855
E: drhowett@eircom.net

Cormac Hughes (M / CMC)
Deloitte
Deloitte & Touche House
29 Earlsfort Terrace
Dublin 2
T: 01 417 2592
F: 01 417 2300
E: cormac.hughes@deloitte.ie

Ruaidhri Hughes (S)
44 Aranleigh Mount
Grange Road
Rathfarnham
Dublin 14
T: 01 495 2050/086 340 8476
E: ru.hughes@yahoo.com

Stephen Hughes (M / CMC)
Deloitte
Deloitte & Touche House
29 Earlsfort Terrace
Dublin 2
T: 01 417 2545
F: 01 417 2300
E: stephen.hughes@deloitte.ie

Christiane Hutchinson (A)
Catalyst Management Partners
    (Irl) Limited
3015 Lake Drive
City Business Park
Dublin 24
T: 01 500 6236 / 086 828 3422
F: 01 500 6201
E: chutch@eircom.net /
    christiane@catalystmp.ie

Tom Hynes (M / CMC)
Deloitte
Deloitte & Touche House
29 Earlsfort Terrace
Dublin 2
T: 01 417 2200
F: 01 417 2300
E: tom.hynes@deloitte.ie
Member, CMC

Ron Immink (M)
BookBuzz
ICELT
Lower Mayor Street
IFSC
Dublin 1
T: 01 853 7329 / 085 100 6307
E: ron@bookbuzz.biz

F = Fellow; M = Member; A = Associate; S = Student; CMC = Certified Management Consultant

Joseph Jackson (S)
Beechwood Avenue
Ballybofey
Co Donegal
T: 074 913 2953 / 087 754 9364
E: jackson@mail.dcu.ie

Liam Jacobs (S)
11 Fairlawns
Saval Park Road
Dalkey
Co Dublin
T: 01 285 9464 / 086 151 0873
E: ljacobs84@hotmail.com

Catriona Jennings (A)
Deloitte
Williamstown
Co Galway
T: 01 417 2698 (W) / 0907 43063 /
    087 633 7680
E: cjennings@deloitte.ie

Guy Johnston (F / CMC)
European Telecommunications
    Management
44 Adelaide Road
Dublin 2
T: 01 676 7666
E: guy@etm.ie

Liam Jones (M / CMC)
Deloitte
Deloitte & Touche House
29 Earlsfort Terrace
Dublin 2
T: 01 417 2828
F: 01 417 2300
E: liam.jones@deloitte.ie

Brian Kealy (A)
Holfeld Plastics Limited
Willow Lodge
Cross Avenue
Blackrock
Co Dublin
T: 01 286 0922
F: 01 286 0546
E: bkealy@holfeld-plastics.com

Anne Keane (S)
Hynestown
Naul
Co Dublin
T: 086 395 3972

Frank Keane (A)
MKO Partners
The Courtyard
Carmanhall Road
Sandyford
Dublin 18
T: 01 293 3450 / 086 859 9202
F: 01 2933410
E: frank.keane@mko.ie

Nerissa Keating (S)
Mallow Road
Kanturk
Co Cork
T: 087 253 3656
E: nerissakeating@gmail.com

John Keely (M)
Advantage Consulting Limited
Eskaroon
Dunderry
Navan
Co Meath
T: 046 36550
F: 046 36550
E: jkeely@iol.ie

Joseph Kelleher (M / CMC)
WMJ Kelleher & Associates
Waterfront Business Centre
No 5 Lapps Quay
Cork
T: 021 485 2929 / 087 813 0350
E: wmjkelleher@eircom.net

Geraldine Kelly (A)
rXi Ventures
39 Bushy Park Road
Rathgar
Dublin 6
T: 01 490 4969 / 087 657 2206
E: gkelly@rxi.ie

Joe Kelly (S)
Dairy Lane
Saintjohns
Castledermot
Co Kildare
T: 087 242 3410

Mark Kenderdine (A)
Bearingpoint
Montague House
Adelaide Road
Dublin 2
T: 086 238 5208
E: mark.kenderdine@
   bearingpoint.com

Niamh Kenny (A)
Exodea Europe Consultancy
1st Floor, *FBD House*
Spa Square
Mallow
Co Cork
T: 022 55961 / 087 686 6879
F: 022 30955
E: niamh@exodea-europe.com

Fawad Khan (S)
113 West Avenue
Parkgate
Frankfield
Cork
T: 021 489 9332 / 085 731 1399
E: fawad@mac.com

John Kilmartin (M / CMC)
Deloitte
Cutteen House
Solohead
Tipperary
Co Tipperary
T: 01 417 2821
E: john.kilmartin@deloitte.ie

F = Fellow; M = Member; A = Associate; S = Student; CMC = Certified Management Consultant

Ronan King (M / CMC)
Amethyst Investments Limited
15 Herbert Place
Dublin 2
T: 01 662 5973
F: 01 676 3736
E: ronan.king@gmail.com

William Kingston (M)
Gerry Kingston & Associates
65 Millview Lawns
Malahide
Co Dublin
T: 01 845 1735
E: gka@eircom.net

Cyril Kirwan (M / CMC)
Cyril Kirwan & Associates
    Limited
6 Maywood Park
Raheny
Dublin 5
T: 01 831 0469
E: ckirwan@indigo.ie

Neeraj Kumar (A)
Bearingpoint
Montague House
Adelaide Road
Dublin 2
T: 01 669 5980 / 086 179 1141
E: neeraj.kumar@
    bearingpoint.com

Gregory Langan (M)
Business Planning &
    Development Limited
57 The Rise
Griffith Avenue
Dublin 9
T: 086 257 0329
F: 01 633 5628
E: greg@barlan.ie

Vincent Langan (M)
IPC - Enterprise Development
    Consultants Limited
Terenure Enterprise Centre
17 Rathfarnham Road
Terenure
Dublin 6W
T: 01 490 2125
E: vbl@tinet.ie

Judith Lanigan (M / CMC)
Deloitte
Deloitte & Touche House
29 Earlsfort Terrace
Dublin 2
T: 01 417 2200 / 087 744 3260
F: 01 417 2300
E: jlanigan@deloitte.ie

Evelyn Larkin (S)
23 Cypress Grove South
Templeogue
Dublin 6W
T: 087 634 2657
E: evelyn.larkin@ucdconnect.ie

Brendan Lawlor (M / CMC)
Gateways
Oldtown
Roundwood
Co Wicklow
T: 01 281 8418 / 087 243 2798
F: 01 281 8418
E: eiroffice@eircom.net

Richard Leahy (S)
Grange
Donohill
Co Tipperary
T: 062 76103 / 087 698 1282
E: richard.leahy.2@student.ucd.ie

Aude Lefievre (S)
2 rue des Rignes
77127 Lieusaint
France
T: 00 33 6 27 19 95 66
E: lefievre.aude@wanadoo.fr

Donal Lehane (M / CMC)
Deloitte
Deloitte & Touche House
29 Earlsfort Terrace
Dublin 2
T: 01 417 2807 / 087 653 6826
F: 01 417 2300
E: dlehane@deloitte.ie

Fiona Leigh (S)
53 St Mobhi Road
Glasnevin
Dublin 9
T: 01 836 7840 / 086 348 4420
E: fiona.leigh@intel.com

Michael Lenahan (F / CMC)
P-E Consulting Group
24 Fitzwilliam Place
Dublin 2
T: 01 676 6453
F: 01 661 4292
E: info@pesearchselect.ie

Simon Lennon (A)
Bearingpoint
Montague House
Adelaide Road
Dublin 2
T: 086 170 9364
E: simon.lennon@
    bearingpoint.com

Billy Linehan (M / CMC)
Linehan & Associates
34 Woodpark
Castleknock
Dublin 15
T: 01 640 5664 / 086 608 6991
F: 00 44 709 235 6679
E: lincar@indigo.ie

Gerard Linnane (A)
Lintur Management Services
Tahoe
Dunguaire West
Kinvara
Co Galway
T: 091 638140 / 086 818 2846
E: lintur@iolfree.ie

F = Fellow; M = Member; A = Associate; S = Student; CMC = Certified Management Consultant

Anthony Loughrey (F / CMC)
AFL Management Consultants
14 King Edward Park
Bray
Co Wicklow
T: 01 282 8963 / 087 273 0475
F: 01 286 0075
E: tonyloughrey@eircom.net

Seamus Lowney (A)
Bearingpoint
Montague House
Adelaide Road
Dublin 2
T: 01 418 1111
E: seamus.lowney@
     bearingpoint.com

Victor Luan (A)
Bearingpoint
Montague House
Adelaide Road
Dublin 2
T: 01 418 1114 / 087 784 3918
E: victor.luan@gmail.com

Eimear Lucey (A)
Deloitte
Deloitte & Touche House
29 Earlsfort Terrace
Dublin 2
T: 01 417 2625 / 086 307 5044
F: 01 417 2300
E: elucey@deloitte.ie

Brendan Lynch (F / CMC)
Brolyn Consultants Limited
73 St Helen's Road
Booterstown
Co Dublin
T: 01 210 9868
F: 01 210 9868
E: blynch@indigo.ie

David Lynch (A)
Deloitte
Deloitte & Touche House
29 Earlsfort Terrace
Dublin 2
T: 01 417 2969
F: 01 417 2300
E: dlynch@deloitte.ie

Kate Lynch (S)
Coolmine House
Saggart
Co Dublin
T: 087 234 7007
E: catriona.lynch@gmail.com

Aoife Lyons (S)
12 Westerton Rise
Dundrum
Dublin 16
T: 01 298 2516 / 086 853 6140
E: efa_lyons@yahoo.co.uk

David Lyons (M / CMC)
Deloitte
Deloitte & Touche House
29 Earlsfort Terrace
Dublin 2
T: 01 417 2830 / 087 213 7547
F: 01 417 2300
E: davlyons@deloitte.ie

F = Fellow; M = Member; A = Associate; S = Student; CMC = Certified Management Consultant

Derek Lyons (A)
Bearingpoint
Montague House
Adelaide Road
Dublin 2
T: 01 418 1216 / 086 858 7885
E: derek.lyons@bearingpoint.com

Kevin MacSweeney (S)
9 Temple Vale
Ballintemple
Cork
T: 021 4294479
E: kevmacsweeny@hotmail.com

Aine Maguire (A)
Persuasion
Guinness Enterprise Centre
Taylor's Lane
Dublin 8
T: 086 815 3041
E: aine@persuasion.ie

Gary Maguire (S)
20 Marlborough Road
Glenageary
Co Dublin
T: 085 716 9507

Elizabeth Mahon (A)
Deloitte
Deloitte & Touche House
29 Earlsfort Terrace
Dublin 2
T: 01 417 2964 / 087 969 0863
F: 01 417 2300
E: emahon@deloitte.ie

Niall Malone (S)
105 Park Avenue
Castleknock
Dublin 15
T: 01 821 1734 / 086 152 3740
E: malone.niall@gmail.com

Bernadette Manning (A)
Refraction
5 The Village Centre
Clane
Co Kildare
T: 045 982446 / 087 985 7141
F: 045 861892
E: refraction@indigo.ie

Paul Manning (M / CMC)
6 Hollybrook Road
Clontarf
Dublin 3
T: 01 833 0876 / 087 990 5920
F: 01 614 5567
E: pmanning@eircom.net

Peter Manning (A)
O'Shea Manning & Company
Ardeevin
Saval Park Road
Dalkey
Co Dublin
T: 01 285 8411 / 087 222 5286
E: pmanning@osheamanning.ie

Christopher Mansfield (A)
Bearingpoint
Montague House
Adelaide Road
Dublin 2
T: 086 179 2010
E: chris.mansfield@
    bearingpoint.com

Diarmuid Marrinan (M / CMC)
Deloitte
Deloitte & Touche House
29 Earlsfort Terrace
Dublin 2
T: 01 417 2876 / 087 911 2817
F: 01 417 2300
E: dmarrinan@deloitte.ie

Manlio Martellucci (S)
24 St Donagh's Road
Donaghmede
Dublin 13
T: 01 867 4046 / 087 753 6642
E: manliomar@hotmail.com

Tom Martin (M / CMC)
Tom Martin & Associates / TMA
Priory House
19 Priory Hall
Stillorgan
Co Dublin
T: 01 283 5252
F: 01 283 5251
E: info@tma.ie

Kilian Maxwell (A)
Bearingpoint
Montague House
Adelaide Road
Dublin 2
T: 01 418 1146 / 01 295 3207
E: kilian.maxwell@
    bearingpoint.com

Willie Maxwell (F)
Europa Academy
Europa Campus
Balheary
Swords
Co Dublin
T: 01 883 9223
F: 01 813 8653
E: w.maxwell@
    acumenprogramme.com

Lucy McCaffrey (M / CMC)
Lucy McCaffrey & Company /
    Latitude
17 Grosvenor House
Pakenham Road
Monkstown
Co Dublin
T: 01 2800716
E: lmcc@iol.ie

Catherine McCaghey (A)
Helix Innovation Partnerships
Old Gasworks Business Park
Kilmorey Street
Newry
Co Down
T: 00 44 28 3026 0700
E: c.mccaghey@helixireland.com

F = Fellow; M = Member; A = Associate; S = Student; CMC = Certified Management Consultant

Clare McCarthy (A)
Bearingpoint
Montague House
Adelaide Road
Dublin 2
T: 086 086 8346 / 01 418 1290
E: clare.mccarthy@
    bearingpoint.com

James McCarthy (A)
Deloitte
Deloitte & Touche House
29 Earlsfort Terrace
Dublin 2
T: 01 417 2973 / 087 911 6976
F: 01 417 2300
E: jmccarthy@deloitte.ie

Justine McCarthy (M / CMC)
Prospectus Limited
4 Kelston Drive
Foxrock
Dublin 18
T: 01 218 0314
E: jmccarthy@prospectus.ie

Emma McConway (S)
3 Millmount Avenue
Drumcondra
Dublin 9
T: 086 351 9921
E: emmconway@hotmail.com

Lauren McCormack (S)
18B Strand Road
Sandymount
Dublin 4
T: 01 716 8934 / 087 203 2669
E: laurynmccormack@gmail.com

Ruairi McDermott (S)
7 Delaford Lawn
Knocklyon Woods
Templeogue
Dublin
T: 01 494 1828 / 087 759 8060
E: ruairimcdermott@yahoo.ie

Gerard McDonough (A)
PricewaterhouseCoopers
One Spencer Dock
North Wall Quay
Dublin 1
T: 01 792 6000
E: gerard.mcdonough@
    ie.pwc.com

John McElearney (M)
Wynston
Churchtown Road Lower
Dublin 14
T: 01 213 5147
E: johnmcelearney@eircom.net

Michael McElroy (M)
Rural Enterprise Development
    Services
Smithboro
Co Monaghan
T: 047 57629
F: 047 57951
E: michael@
    acumenprogramme.com

F = Fellow; M = Member; A = Associate; S = Student; CMC = Certified Management Consultant

Mary McEntee (M)
Zilcom Systems Limited
Charlestown
Tallanstown
Dundalk
Co Louth
T: 041 685 5016
F: 041 685 5366
E: mary.mcentee@zilcom.com

John McGarry (M / CMC)
Ernst & Young
City Quarter
Lapps Quay
Cork
T: 021 480 5700 / 087 833 1076
E: john.mcgarry@ie.ey.com

Peggy McGlynn (A)
Louth County Enterprise Board
Quayside Business Park
Mill Street
Dundalk
Co Louth
T: 042 939 6945 / 087 686 7838
E: pmcglynn@lceb.ie

James McGovern (A)
Fujitsu Services
c/o 30 The Moorings
Malahide
Co Dublin
T: 01 813 6000 (W) / 01 845 3891
E: jim.mcgovern@ie.fujitsu.com

Michael McGrail (M / CMC)
Sagres
12 The Pines
Woodley Park
Kilmacud
Dublin 14
T: 01 298 2211 / 087 246 8656
F: 01 661 5046
E: michael.mcgrail@ireland.com

Lisa McGrath (M / CMC)
Deloitte
Deloitte & Touche House
29 Earlsfort Terrace
Dublin 2
T: 01 417 2872
F: 01 417 2300
E: lmcgrath@deloitte.ie

Marian McGrath (M / CMC)
Deloitte
Deloitte & Touche House
29 Earlsfort Terrace
Dublin 2
T: 01 417 2527
F: 01 417 2300
E: marimcgrath@deloitte.ie

Aidan McHugh (M / CMC)
Deloitte
Deloitte & Touche House
29 Earlsfort Terrace
Dublin 2
T: 01 417 2837 / 087 670 3982
F: 01 417 2300
E: amchugh@deloitte.ie

Gearoid McHugh (S)
93 Foxfield Grove
Raheny
Dublin 5
T: 01 831 2007 / 087 641 9593
E: mcq3180@yahoo.com

Reggie McHugh (M)
61 Bryanstown Village
Drogheda
Co Louth
T: 041 984 6129 / 087 243 0107
E: reg.mchugh@iol.ie

John McInerney (F / CMC)
1 Upper Cherryfield Avenue
Ranelagh
Dublin 6
T: 01 497 6415 / 087 989 0988
F: 01 295 9478
E: johnmcinerney@iol.ie

Kathrina McKenzie (A)
Bearingpoint
Montague House
Adelaide Road
Dublin 2
T: 01 406 3289 / 086 817 1195
E: kathrina.mckenzie@
   bearingpoint.com

Gerry McLarnon (Hon. F)
International Human Resources
   Consultancy
Hemet
48 Castleknock Park
Dublin 15
T: 01 826 2214 / 086 241 7518
F: (01) 826 2259
E: gerrymc@indigo.ie

John McMahon (A)
Bearingpoint
Montague House
Adelaide Road
Dublin 2
T: 086 179 1203 / 01 276 1021
E: john.mcmahon@
   bearingpoint.com

Derrick McManus (M / CMC)
Deloitte
Deloitte & Touche House
29 Earlsfort Terrace
Dublin 2
T: 01 417 2805
F: 01 417 2300
E: derrick.mcmanus@deloitte.ie

John McMillan (A)
PBA Associates Limited
15/A Claremont Road
Howth
Dublin 13
T: 01 839 5678 / 087 263 3022
E: johnbmcmillan@eircom.net

Barbara McNabola (S)
19 Avonmore
Foxrock
Dublin 18
T: 086 240 4706
E: barbaramcnabola@hotmail.com

F = Fellow; M = Member; A = Associate; S = Student; CMC = Certified Management Consultant

Breda McNally (M / CMC)
Training & Evaluation Services
    Limited
42 Southdene
Monkstown Valley
Monkstown
Co Dublin
T: 01 284 3078
F: 01 284 3078
E: trainingandevaluation@
    eircom.net

Jim McQuaid (A)
McArdle Cassidy McQuaid
Lakeview House
27 North Road
Monaghan
T: 047 81022
F: 047 84123
E: info@
    mcardlecassidymcquaid.com

Meabh McSweeney (A)
Bearingpoint
Montague House
Adelaide Road
Dublin 2
T: 086 395 0397 / 01 418 1276

John Melvin (A)
Melvin Consulting
11 The Golf Links
Malahide
Co Dublin
T: 01 845 4404 / 087 240 5197
E: jmelvin@iol.ie

Julie Mernagh (S)
Moorfields House
Wexford
Co Wexford
T: 053 43118 / 086 374 4055
E: mernj@yahoo.com

Adele Miley (S)
Little Roc
Killiney Heath
Killiney
Co Dublin
T: 01 285 7485 / 086 849 2219
E: adelemiley1@hotmail.com

Ailbe Millerick (M / CMC)
ATM Consulting
Cupertino
Violet Hill
Killiney
Co Dublin
T: 01 285 0409
F: 01 285 0409
E: atmconsulting@eircom.net

Luke Mitchell (M / CMC)
Deloitte
Deloitte & Touche House
29 Earlsfort Terrace
Dublin 2
T: 01 417 2824
F: 01 417 2300
E: luke.mitchell@deloitte.ie

Shane Mohan (M / CMC)
Deloitte
Deloitte & Touche House
29 Earlsfort Terrace
Dublin 2
T: 01 417 2543
F: 01 417 2300
E: shane.mohan@deloitte.ie

Subhendu Mohapatra (A)
Bearingpoint
Montague House
Adelaide Road
Dublin 2
T: 086 837 2435 / 086 409 7011
E: subhendu.mohapatra@
    bearingpoint.com

Carmel Moloney (A)
Marketing Centre for Small
    Business
University of Limerick
Castletroy
Limerick
T: 061 202986
F: 061 213196
E: carmel.moloney@ul.ie

Thomas Chris Monks (S)
Corrstown
Chapelmidway
St Margarets
Co Dublin
T: 086 887 4316
E: christopher.monks2@
    mail.dcu.ie

Brendan Morahan (M / CMC)
Deloitte
Deloitte & Touche House
29 Earlsfort Terrace
Dublin 2
T: 01 417 2241 / 087 984 1277
F: 01 417 2300
E: bmorahan@deloitte.ie

Derek Moriarty (M / CMC)
Deloitte
Deloitte & Touche House
29 Earlsfort Terrace
Dublin 2
T: 01 417 2550 / 087 278 7812
F: 01 417 2300
E: dmoriarty@deloitte.ie

Tom Moriarty (F / CMC)
MDR Consulting Limited
19 Elgin Road
Ballsbridge
Dublin 4
T: 01 634 9636 / 086 242 3778
F: 01 2815331
E: tommoriarty@mdrcl.com

Vibeke Morland (S)
74 St Peter's Terrace
Howth
Co Dublin
T: 01 839 4944 / 086 327 8571
E: v_moorland@hotmail.com

F = Fellow; M = Member; A = Associate; S = Student; CMC = Certified Management Consultant

Dominic Mullan (M)
Microtrade Programme / Mullan
    Consulting
18 Mount Argus Grove
Harold's Cross
Dublin 6W
T: 01 497 0577 / 086 381 7888
F: 01 494 8410
E: dominic@
    mullanconsulting.com

Gary Mullane (A)
Bearingpoint
Montague House
Adelaide Road
Dublin 2
T: 01 418 1179 / 086 179 1179
E: gary.mullane@
    bearingpoint.com

Stephen Mulvaney (A)
Deloitte
Deloitte & Touche House
29 Earlsfort Terrace
Dublin 2
T: 01 417 8572 / 087 642 4615
F: 01 417 2300
E: smulvaney@deloitte.ie

Patrick Mulvee (A)
33 Foxrock Avenue
Foxrock
Dublin 18
T: 01 496 2507 (W) / 01 289 6529 /
    087 205 5312
E: patrick.mulvee@yahoo.com

Courtney Murphy (M / CMC)
Courtney Murphy & Associates
25 Applewood Heights
Greystones
Co Wicklow
T: 01 287 4835 / 087 253 0995
F: 01 287 2362
E: murphycj@iol.ie

Darragh Murphy (M / CMC)
Platinum Consulting Group
Ulverton House
Ulverton Road
Dalkey
Co Dublin
T: 01 235 2484
F: 01 2352484
E: pcg@platinum.ie

Mahon Murphy (F / CMC)
Deloitte
Deloitte & Touche House
29 Earlsfort Terrace
Dublin 2
T: 01 417 2200
F: 01 417 2300
E: mahon.murphy@deloitte.ie

Ray Murphy (F / CMC)
Strategic Computing Limited
57 Wynberg Park
Blackrock
Co Dublin
T: 01 230 3817 / 087 280 9276
F: 01 289 8321
E: murphyr@indigo.ie

F = Fellow; M = Member; A = Associate; S = Student; CMC = Certified Management Consultant

Robert Murphy (M / CMC)
Farrell Grant Sparks
Molyneux House
Bride Street
Dublin 8
E: rmurphy@fgs.ie

Simon Murphy (A)
Bearingpoint
Montague House
Adelaide Road
Dublin 2
T: 086 179 1125
E: simon.murphy@
    bearingpoint.com

Michael Murray (A)
SME Business Improvement
    Solutions Limited
57 Athlumney Village
Navan
Co Meath
T: 046 902 3262 / 087 221 9048
E: michaeljm@eircom.net

Tom Murray (M / CMC)
Farrell Grant Sparks
Molyneux House
Bride Street
Dublin 8
T: 01 4182017
E: tmurray@fgs.ie

Will Murray (A)
Bearingpoint
Montague House
Adelaide Road
Dublin 2
T: 086 179 1169 / 01 843 4246
E: will.murray@bearingpoint.com

Ciara Naughton (A)
Apt 1A, *The Bottleworks*
Dermot O'Hurley Avenue
Irishtown
Dublin 4
T: 01 828 0320 / 086 803 2223
F: 01 828 0321
E: cnaughton@
    claritasconsulting.com

Tim Naughton (M / CMC)
Deloitte
Deloitte & Touche House
29 Earlsfort Terrace
Dublin 2
T: 01 417 2915 / 086 894 5888
F: 01 417 2300
E: timnaughton@deloitte.ie

Pat Nolan (M / CMC)
Facit Consulting Limited
Block 1, Blackrock Business Park
Blackrock
Co Dublin
T: 01 288 4609 / 087 251 9973
F: 01 283 3787
E: pat.nolan@facit.ie

Colm Ó Maolmhuire (M)
Column Enterprise & Training
    Support
Aisling
Main Street
Blanchardstown
Dublin 15
T: 01 824 2620 / 087 273 5519
T: 01 824 2620
E: column@eircom.net

F = Fellow; M = Member; A = Associate; S = Student; CMC = Certified Management Consultant

Sean Ó Mochain (A)
Tacsso Teo
Fionn Tuath
Baile Dha Thuile
Co Luimnigh
T: 069 82092 / 086 260 8954
E: tacsso@eircom.net

Barry O'Brien (S)
11 Roselawn
Lucan
Co Dublin
T: 01 628 0906 / 087 623 9889
E: barryobrien606@msn.com

Conor O'Brien (A)
Bearingpoint
Montague House
Adelaide Road
Dublin 2
T: 086 827 2598
E: conor.obrien@
    bearingpoint.com

Ian David O'Brien (A)
Deloitte
Deloitte & Touche House
29 Earlsfort Terrace
Dublin 2
T: 01 417 2806 / 086 408 6957
F: 01 417 2300
E: iobrien@deloitte.ie

Kieran O'Brien (M / CMC)
IMES Consulting Group
PO Box 500594
Dubai
United Arab Emirates
T: 00 971 436 2177
E: kob@imesconsulting.com

Norma O'Brien (S)
Balingowan House
Newcastlewest
Co Limerick
T: 069 62341 / 087 237 0835
E: normaobrien67@hotmail.com

Orlagh O'Brien (S)
18 Dal Riada
Portmarnock
Co Dublin
T: 01 846 3024

Sinead O'Brien (M / CMC)
Deloitte
Deloitte & Touche House
29 Earlsfort Terrace
Dublin 2
T: 01 417 2883
F: 01 417 2300
E: sinead.o'brien@deloitte.ie

Tom O'Brien (S)
Ardbear
Clifden
Co Galway
T: 095 21118 / 086 109 9303
E: thomas.o-brien@ucdconnect.ie

Emer O'Byrne (S)
11 Rathgar Park
Rathgar
Dublin 6
T: 086 860 0185
E: emer.obyrne@infineon.com

F = Fellow; M = Member; A = Associate; S = Student; CMC = Certified Management Consultant

Mark O'Callaghan (A)
Deloitte
City Quarter
Lapps Quay
Cork
T: 01 417 2355 /086 080 1024
E: maocallaghan@deloitte.ie

Rory Conor O'Callaghan (S)
2 Fullers Road
Cork
T: 021 496 3848 / 085 719 8094
E: roryocallaghan@hotmail.com

Gerry O'Carroll (M / CMC)
Watson Wyatt LLP
65/66 Lower Mount St
Dublin 2
T: 01 661 6448
F: 01 676 0818
E: gerry.o'carroll@
    eu.watsonwyatt.com

John O'Connell (S)
Oaktree Lodge
Tivoli Estate
Cork
T: 021 450 0675 / 087 236 5424
E: john.oconnell3@ucdconnect.ie

Tessa O'Connell (A)
Brand-Edge Limited
22 Temple Gardens
Rathmines
Dublin 6
T: 01 496 5110
E: tessa@brand-edge.ie

Ailish O'Connor (A)
OlasIT - Software Training &
    Development
Maple House
Lower Kilmacud Road
Stillorgan
Co Dublin
T: 01 279 0020
F: 01 279 0029
E: ailish.oconnor@olas.ie

David O'Connor (S)
Summer Hill
Tramore
Co Waterford
T: 051 291500 / 086 087 4819
E: tramoredoc@yahoo.co.uk

Ross O'Connor (A)
Deloitte
Deloitte & Touche House
29 Earlsfort Terrace
Dublin 2
T: 01 417 2526 / 087 794 9046
F: 01 417 2300
E: rossoconnor@deloitte.ie

Diarmuid O'Corrbui (M / CMC)
Prospectus Limited
Parkview House
Beech Hill
Clonskeagh
Dublin 4
T: 01 260 3122
F: 01 260 3130
E: strategy@prospectus.ie

F = Fellow; M = Member; A = Associate; S = Student; CMC = Certified Management Consultant

Muireann O'Dea (A)
Bearingpoint
Montague House
Adelaide Road
Dublin 2
T: 086 179 1128
E: muireann.odea@
      bearingpoint.com

Caroline Oden (A)
Deloitte
Deloitte & Touche House
29 Earlsfort Terrace
Dublin 2
T: 01 417 2620 / 086 399 5393
F: 01 417 2300
E: coden@deloitte.ie

Claire O'Donnell (A)
Deloitte
Deloitte & Touche House
29 Earlsfort Terrace
Dublin 2
T: 01 417 2372
F: 01 417 2300
E: claire.odonnell@deloitte.ie

Frank O'Donoghue (M / CMC)
McIver Consulting
49 Upper Mount Street
Dublin 2
T: 01 676 6647
F: 01 661 2528
E: frank.odonoghue@mciver-
      consulting.com

Eoin O'Donovan (M / CMC)
O'Donovan Tate Consulting
      Limited
19 Upper Mount Street, Basement
Dublin 2
T: 01 211 5876
F: 01 676 3814
E: eoinmjodonovan@eircom.net

Patrick O'Driscoll (F / CMC)
P V O'Driscoll & Co Limited
3 Ashboro
Shanakiel
Cork
T: 021 439 6884
F: 021 4396884
E: pvodriscoll@eircom.net

Michael O'Dwyer (A)
Bearingpoint
Montague House
Adelaide Road
Dublin 2
T: 086 179 1189
E: michael.odwyer@
      bearingpoint.com

Michele O'Dwyer (M)
Department of Management /
      College of Business
University of Limerick
Castletroy
Limerick
T: 061 213161
F: 061 213196
E: michele.odwyer@ul.ie

Kevin O'Flanagan (S)
15 Richmond
Newtownpark Avenue
Blackrock
Co Dublin
T: 01 283 1910 / 086 353 3200
E: kevin.oflanagan@ucdconnect.ie

Paul O'Grady (M / CMC)
Prospectus Limited
12 Beaver Row
Donnybrook
Dublin 4
T: 01 218 3802
E: pogrady@prospectus.ie

Raymond O'Hanlon (A)
Barry House
Kenagh
Co Longford
T: 0906 432415
E: rohanlon@
   resultsmanagement.net

Charlie O'Hurley (M / CMC)
O'Hurley Blair Irwin
3rd Floor, *Mount Kennett House*
Henry Street
Limerick
T: 061 401122
F: 061 401 144
E: cohurley@obi.ie

Brian O'Kane (M)
Oak Tree Press
19 Rutland Street
Cork
T: 021 431 3855
F: 021 431 3496
E: brian.okane@oaktreepress.com

David O'Keeffe (M / CMC)
Corporate Development
127 Mount Merrion Avenue
Blackrock
Co Dublin
T: 01 288 9175 / 087 256 6427
F: 01 288 0697
E: dokeeffe@iol.ie

Gerard O'Mahoney (F / CMC)
Deloitte
City Quarter
Lapps Quay
Cork
T: 021 490 7000
F: 021 490 7001
E: gerard.o'mahoney@deloitte.ie

Owen O'Malley (S)
85 Watson Drive
Killiney
Co Dublin
T: 01 285 8601 / 086 805 8425
E: owen.omalley@ucdconnect.ie

Deirdre O'Meara (M / CMC)
Prospectus Limited
15 The Oaks
Stradbrook Hill
Stradbrook
Blackrock
Co Dublin
T: 01 218 0312
E: domara@prospectus.ie

F = Fellow; M = Member; A = Associate; S = Student; CMC = Certified Management Consultant

John Jordan O'Neill (S)
Windrush
Monkstown
Co Cork
T: 086 195 7722
E: oneilljordan@yahoo.com

Linda O'Neill (M / CMC)
Creative Performance Limited
Clark House Business Centre
John's Lane
Naas
Co Kildare
T: 045 881888 / 086 827 3832 / 045
     877627
F: 045 881999
E: lindaoneill@
     creativeperformance.ie

Nick O'Neill (M / CMC)
CSA Group Limited
7 Dundrum Business Park
Windy Arbour
Dublin 15
T: 01 296 4676
E: noneill@csa.ie

Ruairi O'Neill (A)
Deloitte
Deloitte & Touche House
29 Earlsfort Terrace
Dublin 2
T: 01 417 2246 / 087 622 4382 / 056
     776 5134
F: 01 417 2300
E: ruoneill@deloitte.ie

Caroline O'Reilly (A)
Bearingpoint
Montague House
Adelaide Road
Dublin 2
T: 086 170 5052
E: caroline.oreilly@
     bearingpoint.com

Hugh O'Reilly (S)
17 Sycamore Road
Mount Merrion
Co Dublin
T: 01 288 4298 / 085 143 1411
E: oreillyhg@gmail.com

Keelin O'Reilly (M)
26 Temple Court
Palatine Square
Dublin 7
T: 01 670 7962
E: keelinor@eircom.net

Myles O'Reilly (M / CMC)
O'Reilly Consultants
218 Lower Kilmacud Road
Dublin 14
T: 01 296 8744
F: 01 296 8744
E: myles@orc.ie

Bernard O'Rourke (M / CMC)
PERFORM Management
     Consultants
122 Stillorgan Wood
Co Dublin
T: 01 278 0278 / 087 235 7235
F: 01 278 0278
E: bernard.orourke@
     performanceconsulting.ie

F = Fellow; M = Member; A = Associate; S = Student; CMC = Certified Management Consultant

Donal O'Seaghdha (A)
Network Insights Limited
49 Hampton Court
Clontarf
Dublin 3
T: 01 853 1505
F: 01 853 1504
E: dos@networkinsights.ie

Eoin O'Shea (M / CMC)
Institute of Directors in Ireland
Heritage House
Dundrum Office Park
Dublin 14
T: 01 296 4093 / 085 822 8199
F: 01 668 1926
E: eoin@ground.ie

James O'Shea (M / CMC)
James F O'Shea & Co /
    O'Shea.Manning & Co
Ardeevin
Saval Park Road
Dalkey
Co Dublin
T: 01 285 1699
F: 01 386 8422
E: jfoshea@osheamanning.ie

Gillian O'Sullivan (A)
Bearingpoint
Montague House
Adelaide Road
Dublin 2
T: 01 418 1112 /086 179 2007
E: gillian.osullivan@
    bearingpoint.com

John Gary O'Sullivan (M / CMC)
Deloitte
The Captains Terrace
Scilly
Kinsale
Co Cork
T: 021 477 7785 / 086 824 1241
E: gosullivan@deloitte.ie

Michelle O'Sullivan (A)
Deloitte
City Quarter
Lapps Quay
Cork
T: 01 417 2335 / 087 966 5249
E: miosullivan@deloitte.ie

Louise O'Toole (A)
Deloitte
Deloitte & Touche House
29 Earlsfort Terrace
Dublin 2
T: 01 417 2344 / 085 723 5974
F: 01 417 2300
E: lotoole@deloitte.ie

Otuyemi Adewale Otule (M /
    CMC)
Deloitte
Deloitte & Touche House
29 Earlsfort Terrace
Dublin 2
T: 01 417 2333 / 087 998 0140
F: 01 417 2300
E: yotule@deloitte.ie

Marie Parkes (S)
53 Chesterfield
Conyngham Road
Dublin 8

Bill Parkinson (A)
Bearingpoint
Montague House
Adelaide Road
Dublin 2
T: 086 179 1195 / 01 418 1195
E: bill.parkinson@
    bearingpoint.com

John Paton (M / CMC)
Capa Consulting
Meadowhead
Currabinny
Carrigaline
Co Cork
T: 021 437 8583
F: 021 437 8583
E: paton@indigo.ie

Raquel Perez Verdes (S)
The 20 Brokerage
Townsend Street
Dublin 2
T: 085 733 4883
E: kakunperez@yahoo.es

Aidan Pettit (A)
20 Luttrellstown Avenue
Castleknock
Dublin 15
T: 01 828 0321 / 087 989 8794
E: apettit@claritasconsulting.com

John Phelan (M / CMC)
c/o Halcyon Business Solutions
108 Sutton Park
Dublin 13
T: 01 832 4947
E: john.phelan1@ireland.com

John S Pittock (Retired)
Rosomna
Claremont Road
Killiney
Co Dublin
T: 01 284 8898
E: johnspittock@hotmail.com

Austin F Power (M / CMC)
Power Consulting Group
14 Claremont Park
Sandymount
Dublin 4
T: 01 659 9435
F: 01 659 9491
E: auspower@iol.ie

Evan Power (M / CMC)
Deloitte
Apt 72, *Swanward Court*
Parnell Road
Dublin 12
T: 01 417 2963
E: evan.power@deloitte.ie

Patrick Power (M / CMC)
Power Quality Management
    Limited
145 Biscayne
Malahide
Co Dublin
T: 01 845 4965
F: 01 845 2329
E: pqm@eircom.net

Howard Preston (M)
Facilitation & Consultancy
    Services
Knockvicar
Boyle
Co. Roscommon
T: 086 246 2002
E: hpreston@eircom.net

Alan Prout (S)
62 Charlemont
Griffith Avenue
Dublin 9
T: 01 836 8332 / 087 936 2240
E: alanprout@gmail.com

Bryan Quinn (A)
Bearingpoint
Montague House
Adelaide Road
Dublin 2
T: 086 822 3988 / 01 839 4307
E: bryantquinn@yahoo.ie

Ciara Quinn (M / CMC)
Vision Consulting
10 Yewland Terrace
Terenure
Dublin 6
T: 086 836 2677
E: cquinn@vision.com

Paul Raleigh (M / CMC)
Grant Thornton Consulting
    Limited
24-26 City Quay
Dublin 2
T: 01 680 5805
F: 01 680 5806
E: praleigh@gt-irl.com

Anthony John Reeves (S)
Fir-elne
Wingfield
Kilmoney
Bray
Co Wicklow
T: 01 286 1984 / 087 852 0488
E: tony.reeves.2@student.ucd.ie

Michael Regan (M / CMC)
Deloitte
Deloitte & Touche House
29 Earlsfort Terrace
Dublin 2
T: 01 417 2864
F: 01 417 2300
E: michael.regan@deloitte.ie

Matthew Reid (A)
Bearingpoint
Montague House
Adelaide Road
Dublin 2
T: 01 418 1197 / 086 179 1197
E: mattjreid@gmail.com

Dirk Reuter (A)
Bearingpoint
Montague House
Adelaide Road
Dublin 2
T: 01 418 1239 / 086 822 4033
E: dirk.reuter@bearingpoint.com

Ciara Reynolds (M / CMC)
Deloitte
Deloitte & Touche House
29 Earlsfort Terrace
Dublin 2
T: 01 417 2829
F: 01 417 2300
E: cireynolds@deloitte.ie

Ellen Roche (A)
PricewaterhouseCoopers
One Spencer Dock
North Wall Quay
Dublin 1
T: 01 792 6000
E: ellen.roche@ie.pwc.com

Michael Rock (A)
Act Now
13 Forest Park
Swords
Co Dublin
T: 01 840 4439 / 087 768 6069
E: mickrock@actnow.ie

Ronan Rooney (M / CMC)
Deloitte
Deloitte & Touche House
29 Earlsfort Terrace
Dublin 2
T: 01 417 2871
F: 01 417 2300
E: ronan.rooney@deloitte.ie

James Ruane (M / CMC)
Pensa Advisers Limited
38 Woodlands Park
Blackrock
Co Dublin
T: 01 288 0413 / 086 241 4160
E: jimruane@irishbroadband.net

Barry Ryan (M / CMC)
Deloitte
Deloitte & Touche House
29 Earlsfort Terrace
Dublin 2
T: 01 417 2606 / 086 608 7129
F: 01 417 2300
E: barryan@deloitte.ie

Brendan Ryan (A)
Bearingpoint
Montague House
Adelaide Road
Dublin 2
T: 01 418 1133 / 086 179 1133
E: brendan.ryan@
    bearingpoint.com

F = Fellow; M = Member; A = Associate; S = Student; CMC = Certified Management Consultant

Caitriona Ryan (M / CMC)
Deloitte
Deloitte & Touche House
29 Earlsfort Terrace
Dublin 2
T: 01 417 2881
F: 01 417 2300
E: caitriona.ryan@deloitte.ie

Grainne Ryan (M / CMC)
Deloitte
Deloitte & Touche House
29 Earlsfort Terrace
Dublin 2
T: 01 417 2200 / 086 828 1630
F: 01 417 2300
E: gryan@deloitte.ie

James Ryan (A)
ROCG Europe Consulting
7 Dr Croke Place
Clonmel
Co Tipperary
T: 052 34363 / 086 259 7275
F: 0522 29203
E: jimmy.ryan@rocg.com

John Ryan (A)
Deloitte
Deloitte & Touche House
29 Earlsfort Terrace
Dublin 2
T: 087 236 6709 / 01 868 4523
F: 01 417 2300
E: johnryan@deloitte.ie

Michael Ryan (M / CMC)
ORA International Limited
Tickincor
Ardykeohane
Bruff
Co Limerick
T: 061 382 644
F: 061 382700
E: oriain@iol.ie

Suzanne Ryan (M / CMC)
Deloitte
Deloitte & Touche House
29 Earlsfort Terrace
Dublin 2
T: 01 417 2519
F: 01 417 2300
E: suryan@deloitte.ie

Sheena Savage (S)
23 Avondale Lawn
Blackrock
Co Dublin
T: 087 905 5769
E: sheena.savage@gmail.com

Greg Scanlon (A)
Deloitte
Deloitte & Touche House
29 Earlsfort Terrace
Dublin 2
T: 01 417 2657 / 085 770 4217
F: 01 417 2300
E: gscanlon@deloitte.ie

James Scott (S)
6 Holyrood Apartments
Sandymount Avenue
Ballsbridge
Dublin 4
T: 086 857 8885
E: jamesrscott@hotmail.com

James Scott-Lennon (S)
Tudor Lodge
Stradbrook Road
Blackrock
Co Dublin
T: 01 280 6734 / 086 829 6699
E: jscottlennon@gmail.com

Austin Seagrave (M / CMC)
Astron Consulting Limited
7 The Anchorage
Charlotte Quay
Dublin 4
T: 01 6675 510
E: austin@astron.ie

Emma Senior (S)
Beechbrook
Rathronan
Clonmel
Co Tipperary
T: 052 23785 / 086 603 6588
E: esenior@gmail.com

Susannah Sexton (S)
St Anne's
Bray Road
Shankill
Co Dublin
T: 01 282 7359 / 087 251 0209
E: susannah_23@hotmail.com

Patrick Shanley (A)
Telestrategy Limited
Innisfree
Kilmurry
Sixmilebridge
Co Clare
T: 061 367666 / 086 8528899
E: telestrategy@eircom.net

Brian Sharkey (A)
Bearingpoint
Montague House
Adelaide Road
Dublin 2
T: 01 418 1109 / 087 794 6621
E: brianjsharkey@gmail.com

Gerard Shaw (A)
Improve
Ardgillan Cottage
Blackhills
Balrothery
North
Co Dublin
T: 01 690 3913 / 086 225 6765
E: gerry.shaw@improve.ie

Denis Sheehan (M / CMC)
Deloitte
City Quarter
Lapps Quay
Cork
T: 01 417 2334 / 087 246 1515
E: dsheehan@deloitte.ie

Ann Sheehy (A)
Bright Star Marketing
Tir na n-Ean
Killykeen
Co Cavan
T: 049 437 3900 / 086 389 3547
E: ann.sheehy@brightstar.ie

Ronan Sheridan (S)
12 College Park
Castleknock
Dublin 15
T: 01 821 4453 / 087 759 0533
E: ronan.sheridan2@mail.dcu.ie

James Shivnan (A)
6 St Peter's Port
Athlone
Co Westmeath
T: 087 912 0877
E: shivnan@alum.mit.edu

Sinead Smith (M / CMC)
Deloitte
Deloitte & Touche House
29 Earlsfort Terrace
Dublin 2
T: 01 417 2518
F: 01 417 2300
E: sineadsmith@deloitte.ie

Jennifer Smyth (M / CMC)
Jenny Smyth & Associates
21 Fitzwilliam Place
Dublin 2
T: 01 661 9045
F: 01 662 0489
E: jenny@jsa.ie

Greg Sparks (M / CMC)
Farrell Grant Sparks
Molyneux House
Bride Street
Dublin 8
T: 01 418 2004
E: gsparks@fgs.ie

Grainne Stafford (F / CMC)
Friel Stafford
44 Fitzwilliam Place
Dublin 2
T: 01 661 4066 / 087 222 8470
F: 01 661 4145
E: grainne.stafford@
    frielstafford.ie

Noel Sweeney (A)
Tourism & Transport Consult
    International Limited
The Malt House
Grand Canal Quay
Dublin 2
T: 01 670 8833
F: 01 670 8731
E: sweeney@ttc.ie

Georgina Sweetnam (M)
Dun-Laoghaire-Rathdown
    County Enterprise Board
Nutgrove Enterprise Park
Nutgrove Way
Rathfarnham
Dublin 14
T: 01 494 8400
F: 01 494 8410
E: georgina@venturepoint.ie

Patrick Talbot (M / CMC)
Talbot Associates Limited
33 Fitzwilliam Square
Dublin 2
T: 01 669 4704
F: 01 669 4794
E: patricktalbot@eircom.net

Richard Tate (M / CMC)
Richard Tate & Associates
O'Donovan Tate Consulting
19 Upper Mount Street, Basement
Dublin 2
T: 01 676 3814 / 087 243 6878
E: rtate@eircom.net

Aoife Teehan (A)
PricewaterhouseCoopers
One Spencer Dock
North Wall Quay
Dublin 1
T: 01 792 8566
F: 01 792 6000
E: aoife.teehan@ie.pwc.com

Karen-Louise Thamsen (A)
Strandside North
Abbeyside
Dungarvan
Co Waterford
T: 086 811 9791
E: stottrup@eircom.net

John Tiernan (A)
The Essential Learning Team
Carrowkeeran
Murrisk Pier
Westport
Co. Mayo
T: 087 230 9119 / 098 64851
F: 098 64851
E: jtconsultancy@yahoo.co.uk

John Tierney (S)
8 Woodside Drive
Rathfarnham
Dublin 14
T: 01 492 9907 / 086 881 0814
E: tierno_john@hotmail.com

Jennie Timoney (A)
Deloitte
Deloitte & Touche House
29 Earlsfort Terrace
Dublin 2
T: 01 417 8594 / 086 157 7155
F: 01 417 2300
E: jtimoney@deloitte.ie

Riku Anth Tiula (S)
Korkeavuorenkatu 17 C25
00130 Helsinki
Finland
T: 085 144 6591 / 00 358 40 575
     6083
E: riku.tiula@tietoenator.com

Sita Toolan (S)
Glenomena Student Residences
UCD
Belfield
Dublin 4
T: 086 088 9144
E: sita.toolan.2@student.ucd.ie

Siobhan Tuffy (S)
42 Cowper Road
Rathmines
Dublin 6
T: 01 497 7965 / 087 290 7483
E: siobhantuffy@hotmail.com

Michael Tunney (M)
Donegal County Enterprise Board
Enterprise Fund Centre
Ballyraine
Letterkenny
Co. Donegal
T: 074 916 0735
F: 074 916 0783
E: mtunney@donegalenterprise.ie

Shane Twomey (A)
Shane Twomey & Associates
102 Marsham Court
Stilorgan
Co Dublin
T: 01 214 3578 / 086 858 8363
E: shane@twomeyassociate.net

John Vaughan (M / CMC)
Vaughan & Associates
Stratton House
Bishopstown
Cork
T: 021 434 1483
F: 021 434 32862
E: j.vaughan@
     vaughanandassociates.net

Gail Wallace (M / CMC)
Deloitte
58 Taney Road
Dundrum
Dublin 14
T: 01 296 8715 / 087 783 7261
E: gwallace@deloitte.ie

Ciaran Walsh (S)
St Anton
Creggs Road
Ballina
Co Mayo
T: 087 276 0009
E: cwalsh7@gmail.com

David Walsh (M)
Open Minds Diversity
     Consultancy
22 South Frederick Street
Dublin 2
T: 01 674 0000
E: info@diversity.ie

F = Fellow; M = Member; A = Associate; S = Student; CMC = Certified Management Consultant

Deborah Walsh (M / CMC)
Deloitte
Deloitte & Touche House
29 Earlsfort Terrace
Dublin 2
T: 01 417 2200 / 086 841 3386
F: 01 417 2300
E: dwalsh@deloitte.ie

Deirdre Walsh (A)
ChinaGreen
Terenure Enterprise Centre
17 Rathfarnham Road
Terenure
Dublin 6W
T: 087 216 3618 / 01 490 3237
F: 01 490 3238
E: deirdre@chinagreen.ie

Desmond Walsh (M / CMC)
Executive Business Solutions
   Limited
45 Killiney Towers
Killiney
Co Dublin
T: 086 383 9646
E: deswalsh@iol.ie

Tom Walsh (A)
Hay Group (Ireland)
Newmount House
22/24 Mount Street
Dublin 2
T: 086 606 5525
E: tom_walsh@haygroup.com

Derek Walshe (S)
Apt 50, St. John Wells Way
Kilmainham
Dublin 8
T: 087 677 5848
E: derekwalshe@gmail.com

Margaret Ward (M / CMC)
Deloitte
7 Meadowlands
Carrickmacross
Co Monaghan
T: 01 417 2845
E: margaret.ward@deloitte.ie

Padraig Warren (M / CMC)
Chinook Consulting
Clermont
Blackrock
Dundalk
Co Louth
T: 042 932 1107 / 087 2352969
F: 042 932 1044
E: pjwarren@iol.ie

Richard Waters (M / CMC)
Waters Consulting Limited
Baltransna
Ashbourne
Co Meath
T: 01 835 2279
F: 01 835 7537
E: richard@waters.ie

F = Fellow; M = Member; A = Associate; S = Student; CMC = Certified Management Consultant

William Waters (A)
Waters Consulting Limited
Baltransna
Ashbourne
Co Meath
T: 01 835 2279
F: 01 835 2279
E: billy@waters.ie

Clare Paula Watson (S)
23 Glenbourne Grove
Leopardstown Valley
Leopardstown
Dublin 18
T: 086 087 4569
E: bird007_@hotmail.com

Peter Weadack (A)
Business Mentor Limited
51 Foster Terrace
Dublin 3
T: 086 600 9534
E: peter@businessmentor.ie

Alan Whelan (M / CMC)
Ericsson
Global Services Delivery Centre
    Ireland (LMI)
Adelphi Centre
George's Street
Dun Laoghaire
Co Dublin
T: 087 910 1417 / 01 236 2263
E: alan.whelan@ericsson.com

Jane Williams (M / CMC)
The Sia Management Group
    Limited
2 Coolgraney
Clonskeagh
Dublin 14
T: 01 260 7260
F: 01 219 5986
E: jwilliams@thesiagroup.com

Peter Williams (A)
Deloitte
City Quarter
Lapps Quay
Cork
T: 01 417 8521 / 086 868 3860
E: peterwilliams@deloitte.ie

Johanna Wilsdorff (M / CMC)
Deloitte
Deloitte & Touche House
29 Earlsfort Terrace
Dublin 2
T: 01 4172844
F: 01 417 2300
E: jwilsdorff@deloitte.ie

David Winlow (A)
Bearingpoint
Montague House
Adelaide Road
Dublin 2
T: 01 418 1162 / 086 179 1162
E: david.winlow@
    bearingpoint.com

Richard Witt (M / CMC)
Deloitte
Deloitte & Touche House
29 Earlsfort Terrace
Dublin 2
T: 01 417 2523
F: 01 417 2300
E: riwitt@deloitte.ie

Cheryl Anne Woods (S)
26 Lakeside Drive
Belfast BT10 ONU
Northern Ireland
T: 086 177 6546 / 00 44 28 9029
    1912
E: cherylwoods1@hotmail.com

Gillian Wyse (S)
6 Glenart Avenue
Blackrock
Co Dublin
T: 087 980 4974
E: gillian.wyse@ucdconnect.ie

Tom Yeaton (M / CMC)
Yeaton & Associates
19 Elgin Road
Ballsbridge
Dublin 4
T: 01 660 0500
E: tom@yeatonassoc.com

Wing Hrien Yip (S)
127 Woodlands
Navan
Co Meath
T: 046 902 9107 / 087 979 3019
E: winghrienyip@hotmail.com

EXECUTIVE SELECTION CONSULTANCIES ASSOCIATION

The Executive Selection Consultancies Association (ESCA) is the national body representing the major professional executive recruitment consultancies in Ireland.

Closely affiliated to the Institute of Management Consultants and Advisors, ESCA members operate to the same high professional standards, and the organisation is also a constituent member of IBEC.

ESCA companies are retained by leading private and public sector organisations to assist in the recruitment and selection of key senior executives to CEO level through both advertising and direct search, and total confidentiality is guaranteed to both clients and candidates.

Current ESCA member companies are:

- Deloitte Executive Selection.
- Hay Group.
- KPMG Executive Search & Selection.
- MERC Partners.
- P-E Executive Search & Selection.
- PWC Executive Resourcing.

The current chairman of ESCA is Michael Lenahan.

INSTITUTE OF MANAGEMENT CONSULTANTS & ADVISERS

One Spencer Dock
North Wall Quay
Dublin 1, Ireland

www.imca.ie

087 958 2481

16 - 684 KM

4/408   387

Niamh Fitzpatrick
info @ niamhfitzpatrick . com.